YORKSHIRE MEMORIES

DAVID GERRARD

SUTTON PUBLISHING

First published in 1998 by
Sutton Publishing Limited · Phoenix Mill
Thrupp · Stroud · Gloucestershire · GL5 2BU

British Library Cataloguing in Publication Data
A catalogue record for this book is available from the British Library

ISBN 0 7509 1732 6

 ALAN SUTTON™ and SUTTON™ are the
trade marks of Sutton Publishing Limited

Typeset in 11/15 pt Baskerville.
Typesetting and origination by
Sutton Publishing Limited.
Printed in Great Britain by
Butler & Tanner, Frome, Somerset.

Title page: Lealholmside in the North Riding, *c.* 1900. An evocative photograph by Frank Meadow Sutcliffe, Yorkshire's most famous photographer. After a failed attempt to set up as a portrait photographer in Tunbridge Wells, Sutcliffe returned to his native Whitby in 1876. From that year until his retirement in 1923 he produced a stream of memorable pictures distinguished by their technical brilliance and his artist's eye for a striking composition.

Empire Day parade at Sheffield, 1906. The Empire Day movement was only two years old but all across the country, towns and cities were staging spectacular parades and displays like this one.

CONTENTS

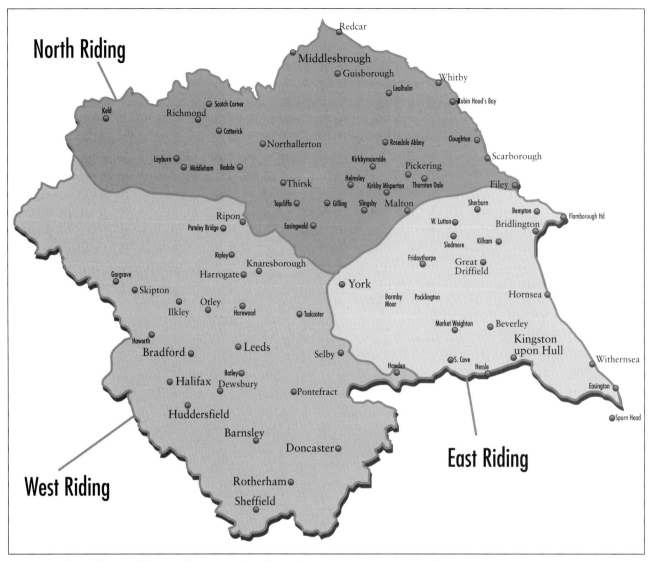

North Riding

Redcar

Middlesbrough

Guisborough

Whitby

Lealholm

Robin Hood's Bay

Keld

Scotch Corner

Richmond

Catterick

Cloughton

Rosedale Abbey

Northallerton

Scarborough

Kirkbymoorside

Pickering

Leyburn

Middleham

Bedale

Helmsley

Kirkby Misperton

Thornton Dale

Filey

Thirsk

Topcliffe

Gilling

Slingsby

Malton

Sherburn

Bempton

Flamborough Hd

Ripon

W. Lutton

Bridlington

Pateley Bridge

Easingwold

Sledmere

Kilham

Ripley

Fridaythorpe

Great Driffield

Gargrave

Knaresborough

Harrogate

York

Skipton

Otley

Hornsea

Ilkley

Harewood

Tadcaster

Barmby Moor

Pocklington

Haworth

Bradford

Leeds

Selby

Market Weighton

Beverley

Kingston upon Hull

Withernsea

Halifax

Batley

Dewsbury

Howden

S. Cave

Hessle

Easington

Huddersfield

Pontefract

Barnsley

Doncaster

East Riding

West Riding

Rotherham

Sheffield

Spurn Head

Map of the old Three Ridings, showing the main towns and other places illustrated in this book.

INTRODUCTION

As commercial photography got into its stride in the late nineteenth century, it was often referred to as the 'Black Art' because the chemicals in use at that time left practitioners with blackened hands and clothes. The term could just as well refer to the ability of photography to conjure up people and events of the past – a genial form of necromancy. In this book, there are more than 250 specimens of the Black Art, capturing unique moments for ever.

They were all taken in Yorkshire from around the time of Queen Victoria's Diamond Jubilee in 1897 to the Coronation of the present Queen in 1953, two great national ceremonials that bracket the most turbulent half-century and the two most devastating wars of modern history. The emphasis in this selection of photographs, however, is placed on the less dramatic, but more enduring and endearing, aspects of life in the old Three Ridings during those years – the immemorial rhythms of agricultural life, the events and entertainments that punctuated the generally drab routine of everyday life, the customs and traditions, the varied scenes to be found in such different environments as the great industrial cities of the West Riding, the maritime communities strung along the east coast from Middlesbrough to Hull and the scattered villages and hamlets of the Dales and Moors.

Yorkshiremen felt an understandable pride in their vast county. They enjoyed telling visitors that there were as many acres in Yorkshire (3,923,359) as there were letters in the Bible (3,566,849) 'and some over'. Its population was twice that of Wales, it had more cities (seven) than any other county, its manufacturing output was 'the great rock of British prosperity' and its cricket team was enjoying its years of greatest glory.

This sprawling area had once been the Danish Kingdom of Deira and it was the Danish leader, Halfdene, in the ninth century who divided it for convenience of government into three parts, or thriddings. The borders he set then remained inviolate until the much-resented tamperings of the 1974 Local Government Act. Middlesbrough was hived off into Cleveland, reducing the North Riding's population by 20 per cent, and Hull was shunted into the short-lived chimera called 'Humberside'. During the period covered by this book, however, the Three Ridings were still in the form established more than a thousand years earlier.

Some of the changes that took place between 1897 and 1953 are not evident in the photographs collected here. The drift to the towns and cities that began with the Industrial Revolution continued during this half-century. In 1851 the population of Swaledale was 6,820; by 1951, that had dropped to 2,088. On the positive side, life expectancy increased dramatically. A man born in 1901 could expect 45.5 years of life, a woman 49. Today, he could count on 75 years, she on 80.

The most obvious change has been in the growth of road traffic. At the turn of the century, it was possible to photograph Victoria Road in Barnsley (p. 150) without a single car in view; by the 1950s, the great open space of the Market Place in Beverley (p. 76) was covered with parked cars. This new mobility was to effect far-reaching changes in the patterns of country life, but in 1953, when this survey ends, even small towns and villages could still boast a blacksmith, a butcher and baker, a grocer's shop and various small businesses such as a carpenter's workshop or a cobbler.

That way of life has now gone for ever but, thanks to the 'Black Art' of photography, we can summon up a wide variety of witnesses to the way we were then.

David Gerrard

PRIDE OF EMPIRE & THE FIRST WORLD WAR

'British and Proud of It!' someone has written on the back of this photograph of young Joe Taylor, ready with Union Flag and toy rifle for an Empire Day parade in Huddersfield in the early years of this century. Empire Day was held on 24 May, Queen Victoria's birthday, and provided a perfect opportunity for spectacular displays and jingoistic speeches. The Empire Day Movement, which organized the first of these events in 1904, lost its momentum after the Second World War and finally disappeared with the establishment of the Commonwealth in 1971.

Victoria, Queen of the United Kingdom of Britain and Ireland, Empress of India, was an improbable symbol of a great Empire. A dumpy figure, little over 5 ft tall, bejowled, her accent still betraying her German ancestry, she had spent more than half her reign as a recluse following the death of Prince Albert in 1861. Sheer longevity perhaps accounts for the fact that, in 1897, the nation nevertheless celebrated her 'sixty glorious years' as Queen with an unprecedented outpouring of admiration and affection.

The people of Yorkshire demonstrated their respect with triumphal arches, processions, 'Public Rejoicings' and countless loyal addresses. The Empire would later extend its dominions even further – following the First World War and the acquisition of former German colonies – but it would never seem as glorious as on that day in June. As the *New York Times* put it at the time, Great Britain 'seems so plainly destined to dominate this planet'.

The statistics have often been repeated but they still astonish: a quarter of the world's population administered by a few thousand civil servants, a global power that built two-thirds of the world's ships and owned half of them, a tiny nation through whose hands passed 20 per cent of world trade. No wonder there are so many statues in Yorkshire of the Great White Queen who symbolized all this prosperity and grandeur.

Two decades later and the calamity of the First World War had undermined the substance, if not the surface splendour, of the Empire. The declaration of war came on 4 August 1914 in the middle of one of the most glorious summers ever known. It was greeted with an enthusiasm impossible to comprehend today, but fervour soon turned to dismay. There was outrage when Scarborough was bombarded by the German Fleet as early as December, 1914, but this was a trifling incident compared with the wholesale carnage that was to follow in Flanders and France which spared few Yorkshire families from bereavement.

At Thirsk, the staid old agricultural machinery firm of Bamlett's found itself 'beating its ploughshares', if not into swords, certainly into gun-carriages. Even more macabre was the War Office commission it received to produce more than $2\frac{1}{2}$ million of the posts used to support the barbed wire that stretched for miles along the front line (p. 15).

When the horrors finally came to an end, more than three-quarters of a million Britons were dead, nearly three times as many as were killed in the Second World War. It is not surprising that most celebrations were delayed until the following year when the Treaty of Versailles, signed on 28 June 1919, brought a formal conclusion to the war. Across Yorkshire people took part in street parties, processions and sports days rejoicing at the end of the 'war to end all wars'.

'Honour from Bondgate' proclaims the arch erected at Ripon for the Diamond Jubilee celebrations of 1897. In addition to the city's official festivities, the Bondgate area organized its own events: tea for 320 children, followed by children's sports and a Punch and Judy Show. Then 650 adults sat down for their own celebration dinner.

As part of Helmsley's Diamond Jubilee celebrations on 22 June 1897, the townspeople organized a competition for the best-decorated cycle. Several of the contestants have also taken the opportunity of appearing in fancy dress. Across the country, thousands of colourful events like this were arranged to mark Queen Victoria's sixty years on the throne. In Huddersfield, the City Council appointed a 'Committee of Public Rejoicings'; more than 2,500 beacon fires burned from Cornwall to Caithness; and at the Pickering Workhouse, the Board of Guardians authorized a special Jubilee Tea for the inmates 'with Double Allowance of Bread, Tea, Sugar and Milk, to finish off with one buttered hot cake each'.

The unveiling of Queen Victoria's statue in Town Hall Square, Sheffield, on 11 May 1905. It replaced an obelisk set up there to mark the Queen's Golden Jubilee of 1887. As traffic in the city centre increased, the statue itself was in turn removed in 1931. In its place appeared what was described as 'an ice-cream kiosk' inside which a police officer was posted. Armed with the kind of 'up-down' signals used on railways, he controlled the traffic pouring into square.

On the moors above Pateley Bridge, a cheerful group of 'Tommies' practise digging trenches. This photograph was taken in 1912, long before the gruesome horrors of trench warfare in Flanders became a reality. This bunch looks pretty healthy, but Army records show that more than one in four volunteers at this time were rejected because they were physically unfit; another 21 per cent were taken on 'conditionally' to see if a few months of Army rations could bring them up to standard. Minimum requirements for an infantry soldier were a height of 5 ft 3 in, a chest measurement of 33 in and a weight of 8 st 3 lb.

The 'Russian Outrage' of 1904 was something of a portent of the much greater catastrophe that began a decade later. On the night of 22 October some fifty Hull trawlers were fishing near the Dogger Bank when they were fired on without warning by ships of the Russian Baltic squadron. The Russians were then at war with Japan and the squadron commander later claimed that he had seen the flashing lights of the trawlers' acetylene lamps and believed that he was being attacked by the Japanese fleet. When he discovered his mistake, however, he made things worse by simply sailing away without finding out whether the trawlermen needed assistance. In fact, two of the fishermen had been killed and a third died later. The 'Russian Outrage' or 'Dogger Bank Incident' incensed public opinion. An international commission investigated the incident and the Russians eventually paid the trawlermen an indemnity of £65,000, considerably less than the £103,830 the fishermen had claimed. The 'Fishermen's Memorial' on the Boulevard at Hull was erected in memory of the three men who lost their lives.

The Empire Day parade in Sheffield on 24 May 1906 – the kind of event in which young Joe Taylor (see p. 7) would have participated. These loyal displays continued to thrive through the 1920s and '30s when the British Empire, enlarged yet further by its acquisition of former German colonies following the First World War, was at its greatest extent and the King still ruled as Emperor of India.

The first 'Military Sunday' was held at York Minster on 19 April 1885 as a memorial to General Gordon of Khartoum and these parades became an annual event across the country. At that time Army regiments still had strong local connections with the area from which they were recruited and on 'Military Sunday' they would parade through the cities or county towns after which they were named. Here, on 16 May 1909, the York Hussars approach the Minster for the Sunday morning service. Local photographers were clearly quick off the mark: this card was posted on the following Thursday by 'Florrie' to her friend Maria Smith. Florrie appears to have been making the most of her holiday in the north as she concludes her message with the words: 'Just off to Stockton feast to have some fun.'

In the First World War horses were still far more important than automobiles for transporting supplies and equipment. Since the Army had insufficient numbers of the beasts to meet the demands of the huge Expeditionary Force, they scoured the country for serviceable animals. Here, outside the Fox & Coney pub at South Cave in the East Riding, an officer supervises the commandeering of horses which would soon exchange their peaceful rural pastures for the hellish conditions of the muddy, shell-pocked fields of the front line.

Outside the Coastguard building in Bridlington, the first batch of the town's volunteers for the war pose with their recruiting officer on the right. At this stage enthusiasm for 'teaching the Hun a lesson he wouldn't forget' was boundless and in the first month of recruitment more than 500,000 men signed on. One of the most popular Music Hall turns was a group of actresses dressed as patriotic mothers singing *We don't want to lose you, but we think you ought to go*. . . . As the war dragged on and newspapers filled their columns with the names of those killed or 'missing in action' in Flanders, the stream of volunteers dried up and in early 1916 it became necessary to introduce conscription.

Miss Hopcott of Huddersfield, 'soldier' in the Land Army. With most able-bodied men now drafted to the Western Front, the country faced an acute shortage of agricultural workers. The Land Army was formed in 1917 to fill this need and by the end of the war some 13,000 women, mostly from the middle and upper classes, had signed on. They were provided with a uniform and paid 15s (75p) a week but could be fined £2 if they left before completing their six- or twelve-month contract.

One of the Leeds trams commandeered as mobile recruiting centres. Flamboyantly decorated, they toured the area urging young men to 'Go Now. Don't Have To Be Fetched'. Inside the tram a military band played stirring martial music as the volunteers queued to sign on. On this tram the centre panel calls for '3000 Recruits from Leeds. British Bulldogs, Airedale or Yorkshire Terriers'.

Land Army workers felling trees in the plantations around Catterick Camp in 1917. The Land Army had three divisions: agricultural, forage (looking after foodstuffs) and tree-felling. None of them was an easy option since all Land Army soldiers were required to work for ten or twelve hours a day, six days a week. Many single women were posted to distant farms where they might find themselves sleeping on the floor of a barn. And despite the fact that they were paid much less than men doing similar work, they encountered a great deal of hostility from men who saw them as a threat to their own employment.

The First World War brought an unexpected surge of business for the agricultural machinery firm, Bamlett's of Thirsk. As well as making gun-carriage parts, Bamlett's was also commissioned to produce more than 2½ million of these metal screw-posts. They were used to support the rolling skeins of barbed wire which became such a gruesome symbol of the futile carnage that cut short the lives of more than three-quarters of a million Britons between 1914 and 1918. Bamlett's, founded in 1878, lasted just over a century before succumbing to the recession of the 1980s.

Scarborough's Submarine Week, March 4th to 9th. 1918.

The National War Bond Campaign came up with some very inventive ideas to raise money for the war effort. The week 4–9 March 1918 was declared 'Scarborough's Submarine Week', and this rather unconvincing mock-up of a German U-boat was parked outside the Pavilion Hotel to help raise the target of £100,000 for building a British counterpart. On the back of this promotional postcard, the campaign's organizers urge: 'Every coin that's in the town / Florin, shilling, or cart-wheel crown / Nimble tanner and humble "brown" / Scrape together and plank 'em down.' (The florin was a 2s [10p] piece, the crown was worth 5s [25p], the tanner 6d [2½p] and the humble 'brown' was a copper penny [0.4p]).

These Children have collected nearly three Pounds for the Prince of Wales' Nat: War Fund in two days.

Fund-raising on a more modest level in Pickering. Armed only with five flags, three drums, two collecting boxes and a pipe, 'These children have collected nearly three pounds for the Prince of Wales' National War Fund in two days'. Their achievement is more impressive than it may seem: £3 in 1916 was equivalent to more than £100 in today's money.

This looks suspiciously like a posed photograph taken on a runway, probably at Hedon airfield near Hull. It is quite true, however, that in the early stages of the war, this was the only method by which the Royal Flying Corps could deliver a bomb. French pilots had introduced the idea by tossing 6 in steel darts, *flechettes*, from the cockpit: British airmen followed this by dropping, or throwing, standard infantry grenades at enemy planes. Military historians all agree that it is most unlikely that a single hostile aircraft suffered any damage from this early form of aerial bombardment.

Richard Thorpe's magnificent steam wagon arrives at Ripon Camp with an impressive load of mail bags for the soldiers billeted there. Ripon remained an important military centre well after the First World War. In 1938, for example, the local paper published an account of a weekend exercise in which 'feigned bandit attacks' on a city garrison were successfully repulsed by other army units.

A group of Tommies outside their tent at Ripon Camp. The picture seems to have been posed to suggest aspects of life at the encampment: the two standing men wearing boxing gloves; the man on the left with the mallet used for setting up the tent; the one on the right hinting what camp cuisine was like with a bayonetted loaf. A postcard sent from here in 1915 grumbles, 'I felt the ground a bit hard last night'.

COUNTRY LIFE

Sharpening the Turf Spade

-R. Hayes-

A turfcutter sharpens his spade at Blakey Ridge, Ryedale, in the 1930s. As fuel, turf was regarded by many as much better than peat. It contained sand which meant that it dried out more quickly, did not shrink as much as peat, gave out more heat and burned with a brighter flame. This turfcutter is using a belly spade. He did not dig the turf but scraped it off by pushing the spade forward from his belly which was protected by the leather and wood 'knapper' hanging from his waist. Unfortunately, I've not been able to discover the identity of this striking figure.

In the years before the First World War one of the most important dates in the agricultural calendar was Michaelmas Day. On that day, farm workers made their way to the nearest market town, each bearing his or her badge of employment – a crook for the shepherd, a mop for the maid. At the Hiring Fair they hoped to find a more congenial employer. It was unlikely that they would be much better paid since wages for a general farmhand varied little from the standard 8*s* (40p) a week, but they could hope for a master who didn't stint on the food provided free for live-in workers.

Many of the trades that were common then – basket-weaving and candle-making, for example – generally survive now only in the protected environment of craft centres: others, like cheese- and butter-making have succumbed in the face of mass production. A casualty of a different kind has been the miles of carefully tended hedgerow that once criss-crossed the Vale of York. Most of them have been ripped out to create larger, machine-friendly fields and consequently larger profits.

Not that there's anything new about the machines. Steam engines like the ones on pp. 22–3 were in use on Yorkshire farms in the 1870s, but this early technology still required a considerable number of humans to service it. Later, more advanced machines, needing progressively fewer people to work them,

would be carefully studied by farmers attending the county's premier agricultural event, the Great Yorkshire Show (pp. 24–5), founded in 1837 and still going strong.

The triumph of machines over quadrupeds is now total, but throughout the half-century surveyed here horses were still very much in evidence, not just on the smaller farms, but at Yorkshire's many racecourses and at the various Hunts whose meetings at that time attracted only appreciative spectators.

For farming people the most demanding taskmaster was the weather. There is no space here to delve into the vast body of folklore that has tried to discern a pattern in the fickle and capricious vagaries of Yorkshire weather, but I have included a number of photographs to illustrate the constant battle with the elements. Unfortunately, no pictures exist of the snow that fell on 8 June 1880 at Silsden Moor, or of the thunderstorm on Ilkley Moor in 1900 that lasted for $7\frac{1}{2}$ hours, still less of the hailstones 5 in in circumference that crashed down on Howarth in 1652. The photographs in this chapter show that extreme weather long pre-dates the effects of global warming, as does the fact that even in an ordinary year 10 per cent of the North Riding's road maintenance budget would be spent on clearing snow, a proportion which could more than double in a severe winter.

The photographer who captured this image in the fields near South Cave in the East Riding was probably attracted primarily by the antiquated but picturesque headwear. Resembling the famous Staithes bonnets, these hand-knitted caps had padded tops making it more comfortable to carry baskets of fish or bait on one's head. They do look charming, but seventy years later one is more likely to be touched by the photograph's evocation of the back-breaking labour endured by agricultural workers at that time.

KIRBYMOORSIDE PLOUGHING COMPETITIONS JAN.27.1921,
- J.W KENDREW 1ST BEST GROOMED TEAM -

No wonder these two fine horses, garlanded with trophies, won 1st Prize for the Best Groomed Team at the Kirkbymoorside Ploughing Competition on 27 January 1931. Their owner, farmer J.W. Kendrew, stands on the extreme right.

Until well into the 1920s virtually every village in Yorkshire of any size could boast its own blacksmith. As well as shoeing horses, they would fix the iron hoops on cart wheels, repair farm and domestic implements, forge tools and items like 'Tidy Betties' (ashtrays for fire grates). At times they would also be called on to shoe cows if a herd was going to be driven some distance. This photograph was taken at Harry Dobson's forge in Kirby Misperton, north of Malton.

At first sight this scene of threshing day at Tofts Farm in Ryedale in the 1930s suggests that the steam engine is lightening the load of the farm-workers. In fact the 9-ton machine was a monster. 'A red tyrant', Thomas Hardy called it, 'which kept up a despotic demand upon the endurance of the farm-workers' muscles and nerves.' The noise made casual conversation impossible and the need to keep the machine supplied with sheaves allowed no respite for hours at a time.

The machine in use here at the Pickering sawmill, unlike the one shown opposite, did improve the workers' lot. It made obsolete the notorious saw pit in which the bottom sawyer worked at an excruciating angle, his lungs becoming encrusted with a film of fine sawdust.

Dairy staff at Court Hill Farm, Farndale, display the day's butter production. Various kinds of churn were used in this time-consuming task: the plunger churn (pushing a plunger vertically down into the churn); the flat table churn shown here; and the more familiar roll-over churn. Production was usually limited to a few pounds at a time but one farmer's wife in Dentdale, Mrs T.J. Middleton, regularly made as much as 170 lb a day. Butter prices plummeted during the Depression years so that it was no longer worth the labour, and farms confined themselves to producing just enough for their own needs.

At the Great Yorkshire Show at Harrogate in 1952, the Princess Royal, Countess of Harewood (on the right), examines the Forestry Commission exhibit. The Princess, the only daughter of King George V and Queen Mary (and bearing a remarkable resemblance to the present Queen), lived just down the road at Harewood House and was extremely popular in the county as Yorkshire's resident Royal. At the moment when this photograph was taken, the lady-in-waiting to the left of the Princess seems to have detected something rather nasty in the shrubbery.

A triple Royal turn-out for the Great Yorkshire Show at Harrogate in 1951. On the right is Queen Mary, wife of George V; in the centre, the Duke of Gloucester, her third son; on the left, the Duchess of Gloucester, formerly the society beauty Lady Alice Montagu-Douglas-Scott. The Princess Royal's close involvement with the Yorkshire Agricultural Society, which organized the show (she was three times President), meant that the event enjoyed a quite disproportionate degree of Royal patronage.

A dignified prize porker, one of those exhibited at the 1933 Great Yorkshire Show held at Middlesbrough, together with its youthful handler. This was the 96th show to be organized by the Yorkshire Agricultural Society. The YAS had been founded in 1837 with the principal object of holding 'an annual Meeting for the Exhibition of Farming Stock, Implements &c. and for the General Promotion of Agriculture'. Its first show took place at York in 1838 and for the next 118 years it was a peripatetic event, circulating around major towns and cities in the three Ridings. The 1951 show, however, was held at the Society's custom-built site at Harrogate, which ever since has been the permanent home for the 3-day spectacular – the YAS modestly advertises it as 'The Greatest Show on Turf'.

Elegantly attired mothers with some magnificent perambulators arrive at Doncaster racecourse for the 1907 St Leger. First run in 1778, the St Leger is flat racing's oldest classic and the last to be run during the season: 'Winter follows close on the tail of the last horse at the Doncaster St Leger meeting'. Well into the early 1950s workers in south Yorkshire took the last week in September (when the race takes place) as a holiday, rather like the Wakes Weeks of the mill towns in the West Riding. The winner of the 1907 St Leger, incidentally, was the favourite, 'Wool Winder', at odds of 11–10.

Stable Lads at Mr Dobson Peacock's Manor House Stables, Middleham. This tiny little town in Wensleydale has been important as a racehorse training centre since the early eighteenth century. Today twelve leading trainers have their stables in and around Middleham and each morning anything up to four hundred horses are exercised on the moors above the town. Between 1948 and 1960 one Middleham trainer, Neville Crump, produced no fewer than three Grand National winners. It was the monks of nearby Jervaulx Abbey who began horsebreeding in the area, one of their many extra-curricular activities which also included the creation of the famous Wensleydale cheese.

The Princess Royal, Countess of Harewood (right) and a companion pause in the village of Harewood. The Princess rode regularly with the Bramham Moor Hunt over territory which was considered a stiff test of horsemanship. The Hunt had been established in the 1720s and the Lascelles family, Earls of Harewood, were its devoted supporters for more than two centuries. Several of them held the title of Master of the Hunt: one of them, the 3rd Earl, was to meet his death while riding with the Hunt in 1857. Note the rather primitive bus on the left, presumably waiting to transport a few villagers to Harrogate and Leeds.

An enthusiastic crowd (with not a hunt saboteur in sight) gathers to watch the Holderness Hunt meet at Tranby Croft in the East Riding on 18 January 1907. Tranby Croft was the home of Arthur Wilson, a Hull shipping magnate who had been Master of the Holderness Hunt between 1878 and 1905. The Holderness and the Bramham Moor Hunts vied for the title of Yorkshire's Premier Hunt, but when that oracle of hunting, 'Nimrod', was asked to express a preference he declined.

Almost every year from the mid-1920s to the mid-1930s, the Pickering area found itself under water. Most of these floods were not caused by melting snow but by heavy summer and early autumn rains. This photograph was taken on 7 September 1927 at Sinnington when traditional horsepower came to the help of a stately saloon car marooned in water almost 2 ft deep. This is just one of the thirty-six postcards of the event that flooded the market soon after.

What fun! The floods that swept through Pickering on 22 May 1932 caused damage estimated at nearly £1 million pounds. For these youngsters enjoying a unique ride through the town, it probably seemed a price worth paying.

DAMAGE CAUSED BY FLOOD THROUGH CLOUDBURST ON WHIT-MONDAY, MAY 29th, 1944.
WOODHEAD ROAD AT VICTORIA, HOLMFIRTH.

This photograph was taken at Holmfirth in the West Riding on Tuesday 30 May 1944. The day before was a holiday, Whit-Monday, and as they enjoyed their day off townspeople had watched a huge, black bank of cloud, 'tinged with purple', massing over their town. Suddenly it burst its waters, causing the kind of damage seen here. Eighty-eight years earlier, in 1852, Holmfirth had suffered an even more disastrous calamity when Bilberry reservoir, just up the dale, broke its banks and 90 million gallons of water cascaded through the town. Nowadays, Holmfirth is best known as the main location for the BBC Television series *Last of the Summer Wine*.

Another picture of the Pickering floods of 1927, this one taken on 25 August. On this occasion, the Pickering to York bus finds itself stranded and the young lad in the row-boat seems to be in possession of the only viable means of transport. With fields under a foot or more of water, the hay harvest that year was a total loss.

Floods at Howe Bridge, Nr Pickering. March 1933.

March 1933 and the Pickering area is flooded once again. This photograph was taken at Howe Bridge where the driver of the Manchester-registered car seems to have travelled well-prepared by carrying a small boat on his roof. A lady on the back seat is peering out rather anxiously. This moment was captured by the distinguished local photographer Sydney Smith, a collection of whose atmospheric pictures of the area can be seen at the Beck Isle Museum in Pickering.

Ironically those spring floods of 1933 were followed by the 'Dryest summer on record' in nearby Newtondale. Workers converged on Pickering Beck to collect water for the scattered villages of the dale. The man on the left is using a bucket fixed to the end of a pole to fill one of the barrels as two youngsters follow the operation with interest. Until well into the 1940s the water-carrier was a familiar sight in the more remote communities of the dales and moors.

Yorkshire shares with Lancashire the British record for the greatest number of electrical storms in a year – Huddersfield in 1967 endured thirty-eight of them in all. A spectacular thunderstorm in July 1907 shattered this ancient tree at Gargrave in Airedale.

As a variation on the floods that inundated Pickering almost every year, a violent hail storm assailed the town on 5 June 1935. The Market Place, shown here, was covered by a layer of hailstones up to 12 in deep. That year 5 June was Derby Day and also the day fixed for the Pickering Sunday School's annual outing to Scarborough.

The winter of 1947 was the worst Yorkshire had experienced since the 'Great Storm' of 1885. There were unprecedentedly heavy snowfalls on 2 February and for the next two months much of the county was paralysed. This car had been abandoned at Lockton in the North York Moors on 22 February by a midwife struggling to get to a home confinement. For weeks walls of snow up to 16 ft high made moorland roads impassable. Thousands of sheep perished in snowdrifts and long stretches of the Settle to Carlisle railway were closed through most of February and March.

This scene was also photographed at Lockton. The bus had been taking thirty-two passengers back to Whitby after a visit to the pantomime at Leeds. Fortunately the bus ground to a halt quite near the Fox and Rabbit Inn at Saltersgate. A note on the back says 'This Bus has been embedded in Snow drifts at Lockton for over a month & still there on March 14th, 1947'. That winter the situation became so critical in the remoter parts of the dales and moors that the RAF was drafted in to drop emergency supplies.

BY SEA & SHORE

Bempton Cliffs, 400 ft high, are the most northerly extremity of the great belt of chalk that runs across England from the Isle of Wight to Flamborough Head. The cliffs provide a perfect nesting place for colonies of guillemots, puffins, fulmars and Britain's largest seabird, the gannet, with a wingspan of 6 ft. In Victorian times crowds gathered to watch gangs of 'climmers' descending the cliffs on a rope to gather the eggs, some for collectors, but most for food. The 'climmers' also slaughtered kittiwakes in their thousands to provide hat feathers and stuffing for mattresses. The first Bird Protection Act of 1869 was specifically designed to protect the kittiwakes at Bempton. Egg collection was not finally banned until 1954.

Renowned for its bracing air, Yorkshire's east coast was an early beneficiary of the nineteenth-century craze for sea bathing. Scarborough, with its historic castle, dramatic setting and fine beaches, was the first to be developed, Filey and Bridlington following shortly afterwards. For the people of Hull, Hornsea was the favoured resort; the mill workers of Middlesbrough flocked to the level sands at Redcar. All of these seaside towns owed their initial success to the North Eastern Railway which advertised them heavily and laid on frequent and inexpensive excursion trains from the major population centres. The NER was not, however, welcomed at Saltburn-by-the-Sea. This custom-built resort, designed for affluent, middle-class holiday-makers, was created in the 1860s by a private company: its directors specifically banned excursion parties from visiting their town's elegant promenades.

Rail-borne tourism along Yorkshire's coast continued to flourish well into the 1950s with visitors crowding the steep, narrow streets of picturesque fishing villages like Robin Hood's Bay, or dutifully struggling up the 199 steps from Whitby harbour to the impressive ruins of the Abbey. Welcome though it was, the income from tourists was far less important to the economy than the more workaday revenues that flowed through the great port of Hull. At the turn of the century the only two British ports which handled more cargo than Hull were London and Liverpool.

Hull was unquestionably Yorkshire's premier commercial port, but the fishing fleets that set sail from Whitby, Scarborough and Bridlington were also prospering. The North Sea then provided an abundant harvest: boats returned to harbour wallowing deep in the water under the weight of their catch. At the subsequent fish auctions prime cod would be knocked down at a few pennies a pound. The great shoals of herring that drifted southwards from early summer were also easy prey: Scottish trawlers pursued them at sea, Scottish fishergirls followed the fleet overland from port to port. Wherever the fishergirls stopped, they amazed onlookers with the speed at which they gutted and trimmed the fish, crammed them into barrels and then smothered them with salt.

Two great claws of land reach out from the East Riding coast. To the north the lofty cliffs of Flamborough Head provide a (not always reliable) protection against North Sea storms for Bridlington Bay. Further south, the contours of Spurn Point get re-arranged after every tempest, but this narrow, low-lying crescent of sand-dunes and desolate fields has gladdened the heart of many a mariner welcoming its shelter as his ship negotiates its entry into the mouth of the River Humber.

A stranded whale drapes itself across a huge area of Cloughton Wyke, a sheltered bay about 4 miles north of Scarborough. The little girl holding her nose (left, front) seems to be the only person here affected by the stench of the decomposing 50-ton Leviathan.

The *Leonora* stranded on the rocks of Bridlington Bay following a storm in January 1905. Sheltered from North Sea tempests by Flamborough Head, Bridlington Bay was known to sailors as the 'Bay of Safety'. This despite the fact that during the nineteenth century at least eighty ships were wrecked here, thirty of them after a terrible storm on 2 February 1871.

The Lighthouse at Withernsea, c. 1922. The 125 ft high lighthouse went out of service in 1976 and has been converted into two contrasting museums. One is dedicated to the work of the Royal National Lifeboat Institution, the other to a Withernsea girl, the actress Kay Kendall (1926–59), who enjoyed great success in London's West End theatres playing in sophisticated comedies, but who is probably best remembered for her rousing trumpet-playing scene in the Ealing Studios film, *Genevieve*.

Corporation horses draw the Easington lifeboat into the waves. Whenever it was necessary to launch the lifeboat, maroons were detonated and the ten horses, wherever they were, were released from their traces and ridden to the lifeboat house. The horses were always given extra food for this duty and so responded eagerly to the sound of the rockets being fired. It was, however, tricky work and occasionally a horse would drown. The lifeboat team itself suffered its worst disaster shortly after this photograph was taken in 1909. Six men perished, three of them while trying to save their companions.

Flither pickers at Howden, *c.* 1903. 'Flither' was the local word for a limpet and limpets were worth collecting because they were highly prized by fishermen as bait. Removing these 'marine gastropod molluscs' from the rocks, to which they attached themselves tenaciously the moment they sensed any danger, required a great deal of patience and a sharp knife.

A winkle-collecting competition at Spurn Point. On this desolate promontory, which curls across the mouth of the Humber, there lived in the 1670s a hermit named Richard Reedbarrow. He began building with his own hands a tower to support a beacon 'that should teach people to hold the right course' into the Humber estuary. Completed with the aid of government funds, it was the first lighthouse in Yorkshire and possibly in England. In the misty background of this picture stands the third lighthouse to be built on that site, in 1895.

The crew of the Hull-registered trawler *CW Jordan*, built in 1907. Crew members participated in the profits from their catch and, although the captain took the largest share, trawlermen enjoyed the possibility of substantial rewards from a heavy catch – especially if they arrived at their home harbour well before their competitors.

St Andrew's Dock, Hull in the late 1930s. There were 7 miles of docks at Hull: St Andrew's, 806 ft long, was used exclusively by Hull's fishing fleet. 'As quickly as their catch can be brought up from the hold – tubs of plaice, turbot, halibut, codfish, ling, hake or herring – it is sold at auction to the fish buyers who attend from all the large towns of the north of England; and as quickly it is packed on board the waiting "Fish Trains" which will distribute it among the 15 million people who live within the reach of the port of Hull.' Although still handling some 13 million tonnes of cargo a year, Hull was now in fifth place after London, Liverpool, Southampton and Glasgow.

This was one of the most photographed scenes in Whitby during the years before 1914 – Scottish fishergirls packing the day's catch into barrels. From early summer shoals of top-quality herring drifted southwards from the Scottish coast; they were followed down the coast by trawlers and on land by bands of Scottish girls whose speed at 'gipping', gutting and trimming the fish, was quite astonishing. Most of them could comfortably deal with 60 fish a minute; some, it was claimed, could dispose of up to 100 in the same time.

Only the names have been changed. The same enchanting ladies who appear on this alluring invitation to visit Bridlington can also be found on scores of similar postcards promoting the attractions of seaside resorts from Berwick all the way around the English coast to Morecambe Bay.

This charming picture of a mother and her two daughters on the beach at Bridlington was taken in 1912. Bridlington was served by the North Eastern Railway which spent a great deal of money promoting its services to the Yorkshire coastal resorts: every compartment of its 1st and 2nd class carriages displayed half-a-dozen neatly framed posters or photographs urging passengers to spend their holidays in such beautiful and healthy surroundings. And as early as 1913, the NER was also offering its customers a one-week, go-anywhere ticket at the bargain rate of 10s 6d (52½p).

A classic portrait of the English on holiday, captured at Scarborough in the early 1920s. Scarborough was the first of Yorkshire's coastal resorts to be developed because it had the most obvious attractions: it enjoyed a spectacular site and a bracing climate, there were two separate beaches where one could indulge the current fad for sea-bathing, and an historic castle. It only needed a good railway service (that was in place by 1845) and a luxury hotel (the Majestic was quite as majestic as one could imagine): the rest would follow. As indeed it did.

A delightful scene on the beach at Bridlington, photographed around 1908. At this time, local by-laws regulating beach clothing varied widely: most of them required that the 'female body should be fully clothed to the elbows and to just above the ankles', males 'from the neck to the upper knee'. There were no directives for children but this toddler is obviously fully clothed, complete with petticoats.

Another classic scene of the British seaside – donkeys waiting for custom on Bridlington's South Beach in the late 1940s.

Bathing tents on Whitby beach, somewhat resembling a military encampment. During the first decade of this century these temporary constructions were gradually replacing the cumbersome wheeled bathing carriages of Victorian times. In the background cranes are at work extending the harbour walls, a major improvement which took place between 1908 and 1914.

Offloading brandy barrels at Scarborough, *c.* 1900. The legitimate trade in brandy was an important one for the town at this time but, just over a century earlier, Scarborough was a favoured port for brandy smugglers. The most notorious was George 'Snooker' Fagg who dominated the trade in contraband goods with the help of his schooner *Kent*, which was armed with sixteen 4-pdr guns. It was only when the revenue men, acting on a tip-off, engaged him in a full-scale sea battle off the coast near Filey that his successful career came to an end.

A few horses are still in evidence as the *Rosalie Stamp* offloads its cargo at Hull in the early 1950s. It is difficult to see what the cargo actually is, but the van drawn up alongside belongs to Pullan & Ward 'Wholesale Grocers, Confectioners and Yeast Merchants'.

A striking photograph taken near the windmill at Cliff Mill, Hessle, c. 1905. The windmill was built in 1810 and remained wind-driven until 1925 when a gas engine was installed. The attractive building, acquired by Beverley Council in 1983, is still there although it is now dwarfed by the north tower of the Humber Bridge.

GROWING UP

Bathtime for a bonny baby in a tin bath at the Dr Barnardo's Home, West Mount, Ripon in the 1940s. West Mount had opened in 1936 as an 'Ever Open Door', offering a refuge for any destitute child who applied for admission. In 1956 West Mount became a home for boys, and in 1975 a centre for children with emotional difficulties. It finally closed in 1978 in accordance with Barnardo's new policy of concentrating its work not in institutions but in community-based projects.

Throughout the years covered in this book children enjoyed a freedom unthinkable today. Until well into the 1920s the main road was a perfectly safe playground and, even in the 1950s, only the most protective parents felt any qualms about allowing their offspring to walk unaccompanied to school. In the countryside children could roam freely for hours without causing concern.

The nuclear family still provided the stable basis of society, although the number of illegitimate births was rising steadily as was, more slowly, the rate of divorce. Juvenile delinquency was a comparatively minor problem, teenage mothers virtually unheard of, drug and alcohol abuse by children unknown.

But the notion that this was a golden age for children has to be modified by the fact that during these years there was an unquestioned acceptance of corporal punishment as an essential element in the process of bringing up one's children. In her autobiography, the novelist Storm Jameson opens a chapter with the words: 'My mother had been thrashing me. Made reckless by my fear of pain, I ran wildly round my bedroom, howling, trying to dodge the cane.' The Jamesons were an impeccably middle-class family living in the smart West Cliff area of Whitby.

At school the terrorization continued. The birch, the rod and the ruler were as much fixtures of the classroom as inkwells and chalk. In public schools senior boys were given authority to administer beatings to younger pupils and, right up until 1948, juvenile crime could be punished by a flogging.

On the positive side, as the century progressed so did an infant's chances of living beyond its first year or two. Free education, which in 1897 ended at the age of twelve, was extended by a further two years in 1914 and again in the Education Act of 1944. Various health programmes operated through the schools – dental examinations, basic check-ups, free milk and, to cope with the perennial problem of head-lice, visits by the 'nit-nurse'.

These were also the years in which youth organizations flourished. Yorkshire provided some of the first Boy Scout and Girl Guide troops, and most towns could boast a Boy's Brigade. Churches and chapels organized Sunday School groups whose annual outings were a high point of the year. For older children, Ramblers Clubs and the ever-expanding Youth Hostel movement offered a healthy and sociable pastime. Few communities in the county were completely without a group of some kind, even if it was only the rather sad Junior Band of Hope whose youthful members were required to take a solemn pledge to 'abstain from beer, wine and all spirituous liquors'.

The Princess Royal, Countess of Harewood, and her eldest son in the grounds of Harewood House in 1919. George succeeded as the 7th Earl in 1948. Harewood House, halfway between Leeds and Harrogate, was built in the 1760s: the dazzling talents of Robert Adam, John Carr, Thomas Chippendale and 'Capability' Brown all combined to create one of the most sumptuous houses in the realm.

The Grammar School, Otley.

Prince Henry's Grammar School at Otley, *c.* 1905. The school was built in 1614 and named after the eldest son of James I, perhaps in the hope of some royal benefaction. Unfortunately, Henry died young and the school had to get by on an annual income of just over £23. It finally closed in 1874 but reopened in new buildings after the First World War. At the time this photograph was taken the grand old building was being used as a corn store; currently, it houses a china shop.

Knaresboro' Castle.

A group of primary school children on an educational visit to Knaresborough Castle in the early 1900s. They would undoubtedly have been told that the castle was built in the 1130s and that one of its first Constables was Hugh de Merville, leader of the four knights who murdered Thomas à Becket in Canterbury Cathedral in 1170. After that outrage all four took refuge here before fleeing abroad. The castle is one of the many hundreds that Oliver Cromwell 'knocked about a bit' following Knaresborough's sturdy but doomed support of the Royalist cause during the Civil War.

A domestic science, or 'housecraft', class in a Bradford school, *c.* 1910. The white-aproned teacher in the centre, beneath the ornate gas-lamp bracket, is instructing the children in the correct method of ironing. Remarkably, all of the students seem to favour using their left hand for this crucial home-making skill. Meanwhile, the boys would be in the woodwork class, struggling to chisel a mortise and tenon joint that actually fitted together.

A gymnastic display at Northallerton Grammar School in the early 1950s. The school was founded in the early fourteenth century and, after a rather undistinguished spell during the 1700s, recovered in Victorian times to gain a reputation as a centre of academic excellence.

The photographs included here of Northallerton Grammar School in the early 1950s (pp. 49–51, 90 and 116) are just some of a large collection discovered in early 1997 in a dusty storage room at the school, now Northallerton College. An exhibition was arranged and former pupils invited to identify themselves and fellow students. Surprisingly, no one was able to recall the name of this determined-looking discus thrower.

Two more scenes from Northallerton Grammar School's Sports Day, probably in 1951. Once again few of the participants have been identified, although it is known that the boy receiving the cup (below) is Bill Johnson.

A group of Girl Guides at Thornton le Dale, c. 1938. Following the phenomenal success of the Scout Association founded by Lord Baden-Powell in 1908, the Girl Guides movement was initiated two years later with Baden-Powell's wife, Lady Olave, and his sister, Agnes, as the leading figures. Guide companies in Yorkshire were among the first to be formed and they are still flourishing today.

A proud choirmaster poses with his youthful band of singers at Wragby, near Pontefract. The message chalked on the blackboard proclaims that this village school choir has just won 'Four First Prizes and Two Second Prizes at the Pontefract Musical Competitions, May 14th, 1907'.

A Marvel of the Age! A curious group of villagers in Kirkby Mills near Pickering gathers around a primitive radio. A note on the back of the photograph gives the date as 23 April (St George's Day) 1924 and says they are 'listening to the King's Voice'. George V was certainly the first British monarch to give a radio broadcast, at Christmas 1932, but I can find no evidence of any earlier message. One possibility is that the King's voice was recorded by the BBC (just two years old) as he opened the British Empire Exhibition in 1924.

A group of Huddersfield girl guides are instructed in the correct use of the telephone by Enoch Hutton, uncle of the legendary cricketer, Len, who was born at nearby Pudsey. Britain's telephone services, with the sole exception of those in Hull, had been nationalized in 1913 and were managed by the General Post Office. (Hull's service is still owned and run by the city.) In 1929, around the time this photograph was taken, the GPO introduced public telephone boxes for the first time – a grand total of twenty-two installations scattered around the country.

An intrepid group of boy scouts photographed outside Sheffield's Midland Station in 1931. They had just returned from an 'expedition' to Algeria, an adventurous enough trip even today so surely quite daunting in 1931. They were all members of the 167th Sheffield Scouts which was based at the city's most famous educational centre, the King Edward VII Grammar School. Yorkshire scouts still embark on these foreign missions. France is the most popular destination but, in the summer of 1997 for example, there were also scout groups making their way to such places as Russia and Romania.

An imaginative photograph taken in Sheffield in the late 1940s to publicize the scouting movement's annual fund-raising exercise, Bob-a-Job Week. Scouts would tour the neighbourhood offering to perform chores such as mowing the lawn or washing the car in return for a contribution to scout funds of a 'bob' – a shilling (5p). The event is now called 'Job Week' and donations are at the discretion of whoever accepts the scout's offer of work. It is not recorded how much was paid for the mammoth cleansing operation shown here.

A central tenet of the scouting philosophy was to instruct children in practical skills. Badges were awarded for a vast range of accomplishments, from camp-fire cooking to competence in sending semaphore signals. At the South Yorkshire Outdoor Activity Centre at Hesley Wood between Sheffield and Barnsley, a young scout receives training in the correct method of chopping timber: feet placed well apart, at a safe distance from the log, arms fully raised to achieve the maximum swing.

World Chief Scout, Lord Robert Baden-Powell, visits the offices of the Sheffield Boy Scouts Association in July 1920. Baden-Powell was first acclaimed as a national hero for his resolute defence of Mafeking during the Boer War of 1899–1900 but went on to achieve a greater, global fame as the founder of the worldwide scouting movement. Another Yorkshire connection: it was Baden-Powell who recognized the moors south of Richmond as an ideal training-ground for perfecting manoeuvres to combat the hit-and-run tactics of the Boers. Catterick Camp is now the most extensive military establishment in Europe.

A hearty meal of sausage and mash being enjoyed by a young lad at a Dr Barnardo's home in the North Riding. The selfless work of Dr Barnardo who, despite living on the brink of bankruptcy throughout his life, never abandoned his early claim that 'no destitute child would ever be refused admission' to his homes, captured people's imagination and their donations. Today Barnardo's are still very active in Yorkshire, not through institutional homes, which they phased out through the 1960s and '70s, but by supporting troubled families in their own homes and in their refuge for children with multiple disabilities at Harrogate.

'Dear Mary, I am now at Ilkley. I am enjoying myself. Please write back. This is a photo of the home which I am at. Please excuse me for not writing before now. This is all from your friend, Ada.' This rather plaintive message was written on the back of this card, postmarked 7 July 1907. The Children's Holiday Home at Highfield, Ilkley, provided summer holidays for children from Leeds and Bradford. The local paper recorded that thirteen girls and six boys, aged between eight and fourteen, attended the home that year. 'They are selected by the Charity Organisation Society and examined by the Medical Officer for Bradford before departure.' The building is still there and until recently was used as a youth centre.

No middle-class home in the first half of this century was complete without a Meccano set. The idea of this educational toy had been conceived by Frank Hornby in 1907 and enjoyed remarkable popularity until well into the 1950s. (Hornby was also responsible for filling many a suburban attic with his model train sets.) An enterprising publisher swiftly discerned a profitable market and the monthly *Meccano Magazine* appeared, inspiring its readers into creating ever more complex constructions. These two boys puzzling over a Meccano instruction manual were photographed at a Dr Barnardo's Home in the North Riding in 1935.

The Infant Welfare Centre at Hutton-le-Hole in Ryedale on 1 September 1936. The centre was another of the many groups organized by local people. They were photographed on a visit to the Ryedale beauty spot of Hutton-le-Hole village.

Childhood ended early in Victorian and Edwardian times. Free education ceased on your twelfth birthday. You counted yourself lucky if you could then find a steady job like this, oiling the machinery in the Rolling Frames Room at Kaye & Stewart's ear-breaking Broadfield Mills at Lockwood, near Huddersfield.

CHURCH, CHAPEL & FAMILY

Little known today even within Yorkshire, the ruins of the Priory at Old Malton were something of a tourist honeypot for Victorian and Edwardian visitors. They came partly to admire the fine Norman doorway with its characteristic zig-zag patterns and beakheads, but also from a sense of religious patriotism: the Gilbertines who built the Priory around 1155 belonged to the only monastic order in Christendom originating entirely in England. The order was established by a Lincolnshire parish priest, St Gilbert of Sempringham, in 1148 – a time when religious communities vied in professing, if not necessarily observing, the most rigorous and self-denying regimes. St Gilbert's more genial and relaxed view of the religious life gives him a good claim to being a spiritual forefather of the present-day Church of England.

For the Church of England, the half-century surveyed in this book saw a slow but steady decline in the numbers of those attending its services, in the social standing of its ministers and in its moral authority. During Victoria's last years one's presence at church was a social obligation for the middle classes and their employees generally found it just as well to be there. (Technically, attendance was also a legal obligation since a forgotten Act of Parliament still specified fines for anyone absent without good reason.)

For children Sunday School generally added to the gloom of a Victorian Sunday, although one little girl recalled attending an East Riding chapel where the preacher, expatiating on the terrors of Hell that awaited disobedient boys and girls, rather over-played his hand. 'The divel is on a long chain', he roared, 'but he can reach you . . . and he can reach YOU . . . and he can reach YOU!' At which the third boy, sitting as far away from the preacher as he could, called out 'Bugger mu'd as well be loose!'

In 1900 some 70 per cent of the population described themselves as 'C. of E.', but it was in the smaller denominations that religious dedication and energy were most apparent. The Salvation Army, for example, which celebrated its 75th anniversary in 1953, waged a highly public war against the social evils of the time and in its Citadels offered the homeless free soup, songs and exhortation.

On the social side churches and chapels provided a focal point for their communities. As well as the choir and Sunday Schools, they also organized Sketching Parties, Sewing Groups, Spelling Bees, Garden Fêtes and sundry outings. Few parishioners would miss the Harvest Festival, the Easter Parade, the Whit-Monday 'Sing' or the Christmas celebrations. And of course, almost everyone attended a religious ceremony at least three times in their life: for their christening, wedding and funeral.

For most of this half-century, the Welfare State was embryonic, the sick and the destitute relying almost entirely on charity to keep them from the dreaded workhouses. It seems incredible now how long these cruel and demeaning institutions survived, based on a philosophy of 'deterring' the poor from being poor – the one at Ripon (p. 70) did not close as a workhouse until 1929 and then continued for more than twenty years as a 'Public Assistance Institution'. Lucky the child who found himself accepted by a charity like Dr Barnardo's whose homes provided a secure, if highly institutionalized, safety-net for orphans or those whose parents were too poor or too ill to look after them. Unlike many other children's charities which would not accept the handicapped or mentally ill, Barnardo's stuck resolutely to its founder's claim that no destitute child would ever be refused admission.

A page from the photograph album of Miss Annie Whitworth, a schoolmistress in Huddersfield in the early years of this century, and a pillar of the Deighton Methodist Chapel. Top left shows her Aunt Clara Ferguson and Uncle Law; top right is identified as her cousin, Lucy Ann Whitworth; bottom left is her mother's cousin, Emma Perry; and bottom right as her uncle, Joe Brummit. The range of relations gives some idea of how far-reaching the Victorian extended family could be.

Two 'soldiers' from Hull's Salvation Army contingent in pensive mood. It is difficult to make out the details of the photograph on the open page of the album but it appears to be a man in uniform with a flag. When this picture was taken in 1903, the Army was celebrating a glorious 25th anniversary. It had established 7,219 Citadels around the country and the average weekly attendance at its meetings was recorded as 1,202,885.

General William Booth of the Salvation Army is rapturously received at Hull during his tour around the country in the summer of 1905. The General had founded the Army in 1878 and its membership grew at an astonishing rate, attracted by the organization's energetic blend of waging war on social evils, such as child prostitution and sweated labour, and its hi-jacking of popular tunes for its evangelical songs. By the turn of the century, there were Salvation Army Citadels in almost every Yorkshire community of any size.

As early as 1893 a letter in the Salvation Army's internal newsletter, *The Officer*, was urging the Army to use the phonograph to record General Booth's 'addresses on Holiness and Holy Ghost exhortations'. Headquarters was quick to respond. Cylinder records of the General's speeches and selections of marches played by Salvation Army bands were soon on sale for 1*s* 6*d* (7½p) each. This Selby 'Sally Army' soldier demonstrates a splendid Edison Standard Phonograph and a comprehensive collection of cylinder rolls. As a correspondent to *The War Cry* declared in 1896, 'The financial and spiritual prospects of these machines are boundless'.

'United, let us sing.' Reverent hymns, popular songs, it didn't matter which as long as one was singing. On most Bank Holidays (Whit Monday in particular for some reason) thousands of people across the county gathered together to raise their voices in song. This particular song-fest took place at Hope Bank near Bradford on Bank Holiday Monday 4 August 1907. 'I sing like a jackdaw', wrote one participant in the event, 'but, praise God, there were larks on every side whose voices, I declare, came with Heaven on their lips.'

The staff of the York Christian Mission to the Deaf and Dumb on their annual excursion, 11 August 1909. On this occasion they chose to visit Monk Fryston, near Selby. Before the founding of the Royal National Institute for the Deaf two years later, the only comfort and assistance available to the deaf and hard-of-hearing was provided by small voluntary groups like this one.

It is difficult now to decide in which year adults decided that they would never again be seen riding on a beach donkey. Perhaps this photograph shows the turning-point. It was taken in August 1891 on Whitby beach when the Dinsdale Chapel Choir came there on their annual excursion. Only the boy on the left of the picture seems perfectly at ease. The mostly glum expressions of the riders vary from 'I'm quite in control, thank you' (lady on the far left) to 'I'll never do this again' (lady on the far right).

In 1935 Potter Hill Methodist Church in Pickering celebrated its fiftieth anniversary. One of the church's many social activities was the Ladies' Sewing Party. To commemorate the event, the sewing party's members were photographed with two of their sewing machines and samples of their handiwork.

One of the Dr Barnardo's Homes in Yorkshire was the Roberts Memorial Home in Ripon which was dedicated to handicapped children. The girl in this early form of hand-pedalled wheelchair was photographed there in 1933. In 1966 Barnardos transferred their activities for the disabled to Harrogate and the home there still provides care for children with multiple disabilities.

An impressive-looking group of old age pensioners in the East Riding village of West Lutton. Old age pensions were first introduced in 1890 and to begin with the amount varied depending on the generosity of the local council. In 1905 an Act of Parliament fixed a standard national rate of 5s (25p) a week.

Two labourers at work repairing the roof at Newton Kyme Church near Tadcaster in 1903. This postcard view of the church had clearly been deliberately chosen by its sender since the message, to a Miss Alderson, reads: 'I hope you will come to Church on Sunday. You are getting a very wicked girl. . . . Come in very good time as "Floaters" has taken a violent fancy for our seat.'

'The Ebinezzer Choir', Rosedale, pose outside their chapel, *c.* 1910. It was more generally known as the Ebenezer Choir. Ebenezer was a popular name for Baptist chapels because of the meaning given to the word in the Old Testament story of Samuel's victory over the Philistines: 'Then Samuel took a stone, and set it up between Mizpah and Shen. He named it Ebenezer, saying, "Thus far has the LORD helped us."'

The Christening Party at Goldsborough House near Leeds in 1923. Queen Mary and the 6th Earl of Harewood lead the procession, followed by King George V and his only daughter, the Princess Royal, Countess of Harewood. They had gathered for the christening of George Henry Hubert Lascelles, now the 7th Earl, who succeeded to the title in 1948.

This ox roast at the Wentworth Woodhouse estate, near Rotherham, on 11 February 1911 was part of the celebrations following the christening of six-week-old Viscount Milton, Peter Fitzwilliam. He was the fifth child, but first son, of the Earl and Countess Fitzwilliam whose splendid home (with the longest façade of any house in England, 600 ft long) can just be made out in the background. The Viscount eventually became the 8th Earl but met a tragic end in 1948 when the light aircraft in which he was travelling with his friend, Kathleen Kennedy (sister of John F. and Robert Kennedy), crashed in the south of France.

The wedding of Mr and Mrs Holmes at Hull in 1906. Apart from the names and the date, I have not been able to discover anything further about this young couple in their splendid Edwardian finery. Clearly Mr and Mrs Holmes did not share the matter-of-fact approach to matrimony shown by the Middlesbrough mill-workers described by Lady Bell in her book *At The Works*. Usually the ceremony would be attended only by the couple and two witnesses. 'After the wedding is over they go back to their own house, and either have a day off and enjoy themselves, or else the man goes straight back to work and the wife to her new home.'

A wedding car to remember with even the wheels covered with bouquets of crêpe. The name on the young lady's sash could be Denison's, Lanison's or some similar name, but trawls through various trade directories have failed to come up with the establishment that conceived this particular advertising gimmick.

The funeral of John Frank JP at Pickering in June 1910. He was a former member of the Pickering Urban District Council and a leading Liberal and Methodist in the town, and therefore his burial in the cemetery on Whitby Road was attended by 'every mark of civic respect and a numerous, sorrowful band of mourners'.

'It is Christmas Day in the workhouse.' A rare photograph taken inside Ripon Workhouse on Christmas Day 1938. Officially it was no longer a workhouse, since these had been abolished in 1929, and it was now a 'Public Assistance Institution & Infirmary'. The old name stuck, however, and the poor and elderly still lived in terror of having to 'go on the parish'. Ripon's workhouse buildings themselves were quite impressive and part of them now houses the Museum of Yorkshire Poor Law presenting a fascinating survey of these detested institutions.

Markets & Services

Barney Coy was a postman for the area around Easington in the East Riding for more than thirty years from 1918. When he began work, you could still post a Christmas card before 6 a.m. on Christmas Day and it would be delivered before the turkey was carved. Barney's territory included the scattered houses on Spurn Point and for these he (and others making deliveries there) made use of the single-track railway built by the Army during the First World War. They travelled along the line using either a sail-driven bogie or one propelled by hand. The track was dismantled in 1951.

We tend to think of consumer power as a late twentieth-century phenomenon, but when did the consumer ever have greater power than in the years before 1914? Groceries would be delivered to your door by a boy on a bike, the milkman would come round with his churn and ladle, the butcher would painstakingly dress your joint just as you wanted it, the bread would still be warm from the baker's oven and for any little difficulties around the house – a broken chair leg or a leaky pipe – there would always be a 'little man' who knew exactly how to fix it.

Itinerant traders plodded across the dales and moors offering services such as knife- and scissor-grinding, or selling a selection of knick-knacks and novelties of every kind, even the latest fashions. One such trader was an old man who travelled from one farmhouse to another selling bottle corks for the home-made beers and lemonades. After a particularly severe winter he was not seen again. The following summer a skeleton was found near Hamer and 'identified by the scattered bottle corks lying around'.

Many autobiographies of the time recall the distinctive aromas of the different shops. Not just in the bakery, but also the rich fragrance of coffee in the grocer's, the tart scents that pervaded the chemist's, the warm smell of leather at the cobbler's, the heady bouquet of wood shavings and glue at the carpenter's. For children, though, nothing could excel the dazzling display in the sweet shop with its sherbert-dabs, aniseed balls at twenty for a penny, or long strings of liquorice, four for a penny.

The nearest thing to a modern supermarket was the Co-op. The origins of the Co-operative Movement go back to the Rochdale Pioneers, twenty-eight working men who in 1844 pooled their resources and opened a shop selling basic household commodities such as flour or sugar. Profits were shared among all those who shopped there. This revolutionary idea of returning a dividend, the 'divvie', to customers proved extremely popular, and by the early years of this century the various co-operative societies claimed that they could provide every thing and every service you would ever need throughout your life. And beyond, since the Co-op also operated a funeral service and an inexpensive insurance scheme to pay for it.

This chapter also includes thumbnail sketches of two Yorkshire shopkeepers who have entered the county's pantheon of local heroes: Harry Ramsden, whose celebrated fish and chip shop at Guiseley still attracts nearly a million customers each year, and Frederick Belmont, who opened Betty's Tea Room in Harrogate in 1919. Its elegant Edwardian decor and the quality of its legendary cakes have survived to the present day.

A busy scene at the rear of T.G. Lyon & Sons Central Stores, Market Weighton, in 1912. The wagons are being loaded with dry goods (including a large box of Sunlight Soap) to be delivered to customers in the surrounding villages. Smaller deliveries would have been made locally by the boy with the bicycle on the right.

The day's dirty linen arrives at Samuel Wade's Excelsior Laundry, Occupation Lane, Pudsey, in the early 1900s. The Excelsior was noted for the crispness of its starched collars, an essential fashion detail for any respectable gentleman of the time. And Samuel Wade was one of the first to provide his staff with the recently invented gas iron. Note the laundry hampers stacked in the doorway.

The impressive fleet of delivery vans used by the Scarborough & District Co-operative Society, *c.* 1936. Dating back to 1844, the Co-operative Movement reached its peak in the years just before and after the Second World War. At that time there were more than a hundred societies, each with many shops, which between them accounted for 20 per cent of the British retail trade. One in four of the population was a member. The separate Co-operative Wholesale Society was a major manufacturer and the Co-operative Party usually had three or four Members of Parliament. Today, although still a significant retailer, the Co-op has only a 5 per cent share of the market.

The staff of Willoughby's Carpentry Shop, Hull, in the early 1930s. With mass production of do-it-yourself kits for almost any piece of furniture still well in the future, this is clearly a thriving enterprise.

Rudd's the Butchers in Hessle Road, Hull, puts on a grand presentation for its 'Xmas Show', 1931. Mr. Rudd, in the centre with his wife and young son, was clearly a patriotic man. 'Buy British' placards are placed in among the dressed chickens and the board offers 'Good Sound Advice – Buy English & Have the Best'. The Rudd family owned four butcher's shops scattered across the city.

Thirsk Market Place, *c.* 1910. This is how it would have looked for most of the week but on market days, Mondays and Saturdays, it was crowded with stalls and wagons. The Market Clock, which is still in place, was put up in 1896 in commemoration of the wedding three years earlier of the Duke of York (later George V) and Princess Mary of Teck. Needless to say, most of this huge open space is now given over to parking.

Beverley's Market Place has also been swamped by cars but retains an air of distinction appropriate for a town that for centuries was the most important in the East Riding. In the background rise the twin towers of the superb Minster, built over the 250 years between 1200 and 1450. The elegant Market Cross in the centre was a gift to the town from its two Members of Parliament in the 1780s.

Mallory's General Store in Hessle Road, Hull, in 1919, with a comprehensive display of ironmongery on show – watering-cans from 2s 3d (11p), tin baths for 3s 5d (17p). Between them, members of the Mallory family owned no fewer than thirty-six shops around the city. Their commercial success, however, did not ensure family harmony. At any one time various branches would either not be on speaking terms or else communicating only through their lawyers.

The village barber at Stonegrave on the edge of the Vale of Pickering attends to a customer. But why does his neighbour stand sentinel with a shotgun? Were there other local barbers clustering at the gate waiting for a chance to get their scissors into those luxuriant whiskers? Even the little boy in the centre looks aggressive.

The scene inside Harry Ramsden's famous fish and chip shop at Guiseley on 7 July 1952. To celebrate his twenty-one years on this site, Harry was offering customers a portion of fish and chips at 1912 prices: 1½d (½p). Between 7 p.m., when the doors opened, and 2.00 a.m., when the last customer in the sit-down restaurant was served, some 100 stones of fish and 200 stones of potatoes were consumed. The evening left Harry £500 out of pocket but generated enormous publicity with even BBC Television covering the event.

Extra police were drafted in to control the crowds, estimated at 10,000, converging on Guiseley that day. People began queuing at noon and by opening time the line stretched back for a mile and a half. Two brass bands and a dance band were engaged to entertain the waiting customers and a spectacular firework display marked the moment when the doors opened at 7 o'clock.

Harry Ramsden's career as the world's most successful fish frier began in Bradford where he was the first to offer a sit-down fish and chip meal. When his wife contracted tuberculosis, he moved his business in 1928 to what was then open country at Guiseley. The white-painted wooden hut, 10 ft by 6 ft, in which he started up is still on the site today. The present building holds its place in the *Guinness Book of Records* as the world's largest fish and chip restaurant, serving nearly 1 million customers a year. Harry retired in 1952, shortly after the celebration shown opposite, and died in 1963.

Nowadays considered something of a gourmet item, oysters were for generations a cheap and plentiful source of food for working people. At Bridlington Harry White's Oyster Saloon in Prince Street, photographed in the 1920s, survived right up until the Second World War. The growing popularity of fish and chips, first introduced from France in the 1860s, and the damage caused to oyster beds by pollution led to the almost total disappearance of establishments like this one.

Frederick Belmont, founder of Bettys Café Tea Room in Harrogate. Swiss-born, Belmont was trained in Paris as a confectioner but decided to seek fame and fortune in England, despite the fact that he could not speak a word of English. He had intended to make for the smart south coast resorts of Eastbourne and Bournemouth, but in London he boarded the wrong train and found himself in the depths of Yorkshire. The unspoilt countryside and the fresh air reminded him of his native Switzerland, so he decided to stay. He opened his first Bettys Café Tea Room in 1919 and the venture was an immediate success.

The inviting interior of Bettys Café in Cambridge Crescent, Harrogate, in the early 1920s. From the in-house bakery on the fourth floor delicious aromas of freshly-baked bread and cakes drifted down to the tea-room and shop. In 1922 a new bakery was built at Starbeck, complete with its own orchard, to meet the growing demand for Bettys range of cakes, chocolate and bread. Almost eighty years after the first café was opened the identity of the original Betty remains a family secret. Many names have been canvassed, among them that of the Queen Mother. Others claim that during the first board meeting, when the café's name was being discussed, a little girl in the family wandered into the room: her name was Betty Rose.

The landlord of the Horse Shoe Inn, Levisham, and his family. This photograph was sent as a Christmas card in 1910 to the landlord of the Sun Inn at Normanby. The practice of sending family portraits as Christmas or New Year greetings enjoyed a great vogue among middle-class families from the early 1900s up until the outbreak of the First World War. The custom of leaving *cartes de visite* bearing one's photograph also died out around this time.

Protection for the driver against the weather was clearly not a consideration when this delivery wagon went into service in the 1920s. The photograph was taken outside John Smith's famous brewery at Tadcaster. The Romans were the first to exploit the springs of excellent water beside the River Wharfe here. They named their settlement Calcaria after the limestone that filtered the water naturally. By 1341, the town was well established as an important centre for brewing, and today John Smith's brewery alone produces around 1½ million barrels of beer each year.

Landlord William Harland at the front door of the Queen's Head Inn at Thirsk, *c.* 1910. This one-room hostelry, with a back room used as a cellar, was typical of scores of working-men's pubs at the time. The Inn was better known to locals as the Ramping Cat, believed to be a disloyal reference to the Queen after whose head the pub was named: Catherine ('Cat') of Braganza, neglected wife of Charles II, who became 'ramping' (shrewish) at his constant infidelities. Or the locals may have been thinking of the landlady. Or the pub's tom cat (another meaning of 'ramping' was 'going about in a loose, immodest way'). The building is now a private house and has been transformed out of all recognition.

A magnificent steam wagon of 1918 loaded with barrels of beer and bottled drinks from John Smith's Tadcaster brewery. John Smith (1823–79) had taken over a run-down brewery in 1847 when he was just twenty-four years old. Public taste was turning away from the murky brews of the past and John Smith ensured that his beers were clear of any extraneous matter, an important consideration since most pubs were now abandoning their pewter or pottery mugs in favour of glasses. The brewery remained in the family until 1953 when it became a public company: it is now part of the Foster's Brewing Group.

HEALTH, WELFARE
& SAFETY

A sardonic caption on this postcard reads: 'Willie Clarke of Nawton & Residence.' (Nawton is a small village near Helmsley.) Housing conditions around the turn of the century could certainly leave a great deal to be desired but was this photograph just a joke, or did the sprucely attired Mr Clarke really live in this tumbledown house? The Post Office Directories and the Kelly's Directories of the time confirm that a 'William Clark, cattle dealer & cowkeeper' lived in Nawton from at least 1879 to 1905 but none of them gives an address.

As late as October 1932 there was a typhoid epidemic at Malton in the course of which 274 people fell seriously ill and 25 died. Thirty years earlier, the Army was rejecting 25 per cent of potential recruits because they were unfit for service. The average height of the British working man in 1900 was 5 ft 5 in. Three random statistics which, along with a huge body of other evidence, all show that ours was not a healthy nation during the first half of this century.

Great efforts had been made during the 1860s to install sewerage systems in Yorkshire's cities, but by the end of the century they had been overwhelmed by the continuing drift of country people into the towns. After each outbreak of cholera or typhoid the Medical Officer of Health's Report would relate the same melancholy details of whole districts where every backyard had its noisome heap composed in roughly equal parts of human excreta and 'ash', a euphemism for fire ash and household waste.

Victorian and Edwardian England was not indifferent to the consequences of this appalling state of affairs. Across Yorkshire there were innumerable charity hospitals, 'fever' institutions, isolation hospitals and convalescent homes. They were well intentioned and well run by the standards of the time, but quite inadequate to deal with the problem posed by insanitary housing conditions. At the time of Elizabeth II's Coronation in 1953 the vast majority of her working-class subjects were still using outdoor privies.

Concurrently Yorkshire's spa towns were enjoying their most prosperous years. At Ilkley, Bridlington and Harrogate a steady stream of visitors arrived, many of them looking forward quite as much to the prospect of mingling with good society as to the possibility of any medical benefit. Harrogate was the most favoured spa, not just because you could be fairly sure of brushing against the shoulder of some obscure European prince in the crowded Winter Garden's pavilion, but also because the sulphurous waters there were indisputably the most disgusting to both nose and palate and so generally regarded as the most efficacious.

Another group of photographs in this chapter reflects the ever-present danger of fire. The Victorians had introduced publicly funded fire brigades and, understandably, had based them in the main centres of population where the risk was greatest. So when Duncombe Park in 1895 and Sledmere House in 1911, both surrounded by thousands of acres of their own grounds, went up in flames it was a long while before the horse-drawn fire engines arrived, in both cases too late.

Many other stately homes learnt from that lesson and set up their own fire brigades. Far ahead of them were Yorkshire breweries like John Smith's in Tadcaster, who had their own trained fire-fighters in-house as early as the 1860s.

An interesting insight into how ice-cream was made in the 1930s. 'G. Portores for Quality Ices' says the advertising slogan on the banner leaning against the centre post. The ceiling appears to be colonized by growths of a dubious nature and hanging on the wall, upper right, is the bicycle with which Mr Portores presumably transported his ice-creams around the city of Hull. He must have regretted agreeing to this picture being taken since the photographer was actually a City Health Inspector and Mr Portores' business was subsequently closed down on health grounds.

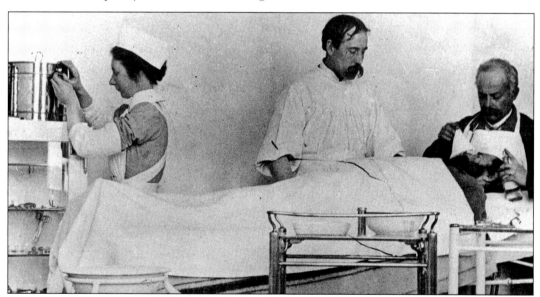

One wishes him well, this unidentified patient undergoing an unspecified operation in a hospital, believed to be Selby, *c.* 1922. The anaesthetist on the right appears to be administering chloroform on a cloth. At least he was in a proper hospital. In her book *Five Generations of a Whitby Medical Family*, Brenda H. English recalls that in the early years of this century it was quite normal to carry out operations in the patient's own home. 'The folding operating table was set up in front of the kitchen fire, the instruments placed in lysol, and cotton wool swabs in a bowl of boiled water. . . . Almost all emergencies and major operations were carried out in this way, strangely enough usually with satisfactory results.'

A housewife collects water from the spring at Gilling East, near Ampleforth, *c.* 1908. The larger towns and cities organized their own water supplies but smaller communities were dependent on the parish pump, local streams and ponds. It was not until the 1945 Labour government nationalized the water supply companies that piped water began to reach the villages and hamlets of the Yorkshire Dales and Moors.

Mr Sam Castle on his rounds at Huddersfield in the early 1900s. The barrel contains human urine which he collected from private homes and then delivered to the woollen mills. There the ammonia was extracted and used as a cleaning agent. Shortly after coming across this photograph, I read Paul Theroux's account of visiting a town in central China where the local people each morning take buckets of urine to huge tanks. The liquid is used for the same purpose as in Huddersfield ninety years earlier.

A room in the Cottage Hospital at Whitby in 1905. The phasing-out of these inviting little hospitals is one of the more regrettable consequences of the National Health Service's policy of concentrating medical care in ever larger complexes. Whitby Hospital at this time had just three surgical beds.

In a beautiful location beside the River Nidd, Castlehead Hydro was one of many such hydropathic establishments at Pateley Bridge around 1905. A riverside walk from the centre of the town still leads to this spot, about a mile to the south, but the bridge and the house itself are now in private hands.

The Children's Ward at Sheffield Hospital, Christmas 1914. This postcard was sent a few weeks later to Bandsman Arthur Siddall, serving with the 7th Worcestershire Regiment, by his wife. Their son Fred had been in that very ward over Christmas but was now safely home. In a rather saucy postscript, Mrs Siddall reminds her husband of their 'fabric' (eighth) wedding anniversary, adding, 'Tut! tut! Stand Back. Naughty!' She sends love from their four children.

Promenade time outside the New Spa Theatre and Opera House at Bridlington shortly after its re-opening by the noted thespian Mrs Beerbohm Tree in July 1907. Its predecessor had been destroyed by fire the year before. Privately owned, the complex ran into financial difficulties and was bought by the Town Council in 1919 for £16,000.

This is one of a series of droll postcards published in the early 1900s satirizing the 'taking of the waters' at Harrogate. As one late-Victorian visitor noted, 'It is curious to observe the various effects which these draughts produce upon the countenances of those who partake of them. Disgust is expressed in a thousand ludicrous ways, and those who have accomplished the task may be generally observed consoling themselves with the somewhat uncharitable contemplation of the ludicrous distress of others.' The recommended length of treatment was three weeks and as late as 1926 1,500 glasses of the water were being dispensed every day.

5—" Nothing, when you're used to it !"
DRINKING THE WATERS AT HARROGATE.

The Royal Baths Winter Garden at Harrogate in the early 1900s. Opened on 23 July 1897 by the Duke of Cambridge, the Winter Garden became the centre of social life in the town. During these years before the First World War the spa enjoyed its greatest popularity, with some 60,000 visitors a year sampling the waters and undergoing such treatments as sulphur baths or poultices of 'fango', the local term for hot mud facepacks.

It is difficult to quite put one's finger on it, but there's something about the kitchen of Northallerton Grammar School in the early 1950s that would surely make a present-day health inspector a mite suspicious. That is probably most unfair to Mrs Bishton, in the centre holding a large whisk, who was the senior cook at the school.

Mr Arthur Arrand (on the right), the French teacher at Northallerton Grammar School, supervises the daily distribution of free milk. Each pupil received half a pint. The practice was instituted by the post-war Labour government concerned by the alarmingly low standards of health among schoolchildren. As Education Secretary in the early 1970s, Margaret Thatcher withdrew the subsidy, thus earning herself the opprobrious nickname of 'Milk Snatcher'.

Ilkley was known as the 'Heather Spa', famous for its 'pure and elastic air' (excellent for TB sufferers) and for its waters which 'burst from a rocky mountainside at 60 gallons in a minute, at 47 °F, brilliantly limpid and crystal, and tasting like Malvern water'. At Ilkley, unlike Harrogate, drinking the waters was considered less efficacious than total immersion or 'application of the douche to any diseased parts of the body or limb'. Ardenlea was one of the many convalescent homes at Ilkley. Its patients were photographed on 26 June 1924, seemingly after a game of bowls. (A curious little scene on the left, where a man is offering a coin to a diminutive figure in police uniform.)

David Lloyd George speaking in support of the Liberal candidate, J. Ramsey-Muir, at Smiddy Hill, Pickering, on 1 May 1931. As Chancellor of the Exchequer from 1908 to 1915 the 'Welsh Wizard' had introduced the Old Age Pensions Act and the National Insurance Act, measures which gave a modest level of support to the ill, the elderly and the unemployed. These Acts were popular with the working classes, but his controversial concession of the Irish Free State led to the collapse of the Liberal Party in the 1922 General Election. This May by-election at Pickering was followed in August that year by a General Election which resulted in the formation of Ramsay MacDonald's Coalition government.

Household and estate workers (and a horse) gather outside the gutted north wing of Duncombe Park, near Helmsley, after the disastrous fire of 1895. They had spent the previous night rescuing what treasures they could from this stately eighteenth-century mansion. The north wing was the only habitable part of the great house to escape an earlier fire in 1879 and, although the Earl of Feversham immediately began rebuilding, the financial burden eventually forced him to lease out the house as a preparatory school for girls. It was not until 1986 that the Feversham family were able to return to their ancestral home. Impeccably restored, the house and grounds are now open to the public.

The brewing process has always presented a high risk of fire, so most breweries trained teams of workers in firefighting skills. This in-house brigade was photographed at John Smith's Tadcaster brewery in the early 1900s. As production techniques improved, the danger of fire receded. But as late as 1952 the John Smith's brewery at Wath-on-Dearne, near Rotherham, was badly damaged by a blaze. The destruction might have been worse 'if the heat of the fire had not melted the plates on the liquor tank high up in the building and out gushed the liquor to dampen down the flames'.

Another historic eighteenth-century house, Sledmere House, ravaged by fire on 23 May 1911. 'The scene on the lawn was as remarkable as it was pathetic. Furniture and fittings, rare pieces of china, beautifully painted doors taken from their hinges, valuable pictures and other treasures, lay strewn around as they had been hastily brought from the blazing interior.' Sledmere's owner, Sir Tatton Sykes, then eighty-five years old, 'followed the progress of the conflagration from an armchair placed for him on the lawn'. Sir Tatton could have stepped from the pages of a novel by R.S. Surtees, a man passionately addicted to the sporting trinity of huntin', shootin' and fishin' but also a considerate landlord, loved and respected by the many tenants on his extensive estates.

Sir Tatton was enjoying his favourite lunchtime dessert of rice pudding when a servant rushed in with news of the fire and urged him to leave the house. 'First, I must finish my pudding, finish my pudding,' he declared, and did so. Messages were despatched to Malton and to Driffield for fire brigades and, half-an-hour later, Supt Wilson of the Malton Fire Brigade arrived by motor-car bringing a supply of hose. Household staff attempted to douse the fire but the water pressure was insufficient. At 2.30 p.m. the Malton and Norton Fire Brigade arrived – possibly the very vehicle and crew shown in this photograph. But by then the damage had been done and most of Sledmere's priceless library had been destroyed. However, the house was quickly restored and the Sykes family are still in residence.

A thickly gloved officer of the Port of Hull Authority removes two of the less acceptable catches from a trawler in the 1940s. Canal boats suffered even more from these pests. In *A Life on the Humber* Harry Fletcher remembers that 'We spent a lot of our time catapulting at rats under the landing-stages. They were the biggest I have ever seen, as big as large cats, and at night when we were in bed we could hear them running about the decks'.

A cheerful 'dustie-man' with Hull Corporation around 1913 prepares to collect the day's waste.

HIGH DAYS & HOLIDAYS

This gallant troupe was known as Wight's Riders and the photograph was taken as they performed at the Great Yorkshire Show at Halifax in 1938. Sadly that is all I have been able to discover about them; even the Show's own programme for that year fails to give them a mention.

Keld is a tiny village deep in Upper Swaledale, submerged from sight by the deep folds of the north Pennines. In the 1930s fewer than two hundred people lived there but that didn't stop them from providing their own entertainment. In their classic book *Swaledale*, published in 1934, Ella Pontefract and Marie Hartley recorded some of the village activities. In the spring, for example, there was always a 'May Stir' and at the beginning of November, an 'Autumn Stir, generally a concert with a supper and dance to follow'.

The most important 'Stir', however, was the Keld Sports Day, held in June, a time of year when the nights here can be as short as two hours. In addition to the usual races and the tug-of-war, sheepdog trials had been introduced in 1932, and there were also less familiar events such as the 'pipe-smoking' contest: 'The men sat on a wall and were given a clay pipe filled with cut-up twist tobacco. At a given signal they all lit up and the prize went to the one who could make the tobacco last the longest without letting it go out. The facial expressions of the competitors as they tried to draw life into a dead wad of tobacco would bring shrieks of delight from the spectators.'

The village's own band entertained as often as the bandmaster could drag the musicians away from their game of quoits, an obsession throughout the Dales during these years, and in the tea tent the village ladies dispensed home-made bread, cakes and pastries. Keld was far from unique. A little further down the dale, the scarcely larger village of Muker held its own full-scale agricultural show every September, again with its own band in attendance. Similar jollifications took place across the county on May Day and Whit Monday.

Until the Bank Holidays Act of 1871 workers had no legal right to any holiday at all: for most, even Christmas Day was a normal working day. And it was not until just before the Second World War that workers were guaranteed one week's paid holiday a year. A Canadian entrepreneur who had arrived in England with £5 saw the opportunities and in 1936 Billy Butlin opened his first Luxury Holiday Camp at Skegness, soon to be followed by others at Clacton and Filey. For the equivalent of a week's pay, around £3.50, visitors to Butlin's Camps had their own private chalet with running hot and cold water, three meals a day and non-stop entertainment. Such amenities contrasted very favourably with those offered by boarding-house landladies who required their guests to leave immediately after breakfast and not return until the evening meal was on the table. It is not surprising that for almost three decades after the war Butlin and his imitators dominated the domestic holiday market.

An Edwardian milliner's dream of heaven! This gorgeous display of head-wear was worn by the catering staff at Kirkdale Manor's Garden Fête in the summer of 1912. The manor, about 2 miles west of Kirkbymoorside, was then a private house and is now a school.

Club Feast Day, 28 June 1907, at Fridaythorpe, a tiny village in the Yorkshire Wolds. Despite its minuscule population it nevertheless managed to get together a brass band and a small number of men and boys for a procession. The event was probably organized by the Heart & Hand Lodge of the Oddfellows Manchester Unity, No. 8272, which was active in the village around this time.

To judge from the expressions on the faces of the ladies in the front row, this Wesleyan Garden Party was not the merriest of occasions. It took place at Southlands, Kirkbymoorside, on 16 July 1932.

Pockley is another small village, just on the edge of the North York Moors. For the Pockley Show in 1904 local people had travelled a couple of miles up Howl Dale to the grounds of Nawton Tower. This was now the home of the 3rd Earl of Feversham who moved here after the fire of 1895 had made his ancestral home, Duncombe Park, uninhabitable (see p. 92).

From the 1890s until 1914 a popular form of mass entertainment was the Pageant. Pageants were often quite elaborate with a numerous cast, appropriately costumed, depicting historical events that had occurred in the area. This one, held at Woodsome Hall, just outside Huddersfield, on 5 September 1908, had the slightly different theme of 'Old Sports and Pastimes'. The tableau shown here represents the 'Crowning of the May Queen'.

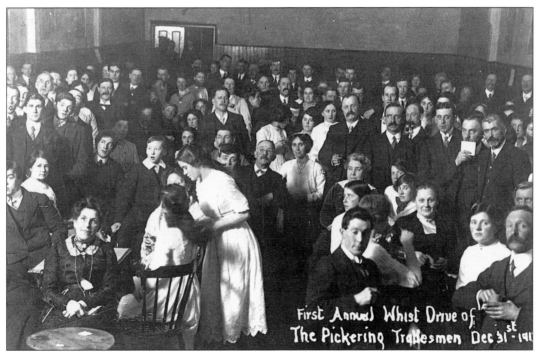

The tradesmen of Pickering and their guests prepare to celebrate New Year's Eve, 31 December 1913, with their 'First Annual Whist Drive'. Whist Drives enjoyed great popularity until the advent of television, providing an agreeable social occasion and a painless way of raising funds for village amenities or local charities.

ACE-DAY SPORTS AT ULLEY

The formal end of the First World War came with the signing of the Treaty of Versailles on 28 June 1919. The occasion was celebrated with a variety of events across the country. At Ulley, a village south of Rotherham, the festivities for Peace Day took the form of a sports day held on 19 July. The lady in the centre seems to be taking the tug-of-war contest rather seriously.

Another Peace Day celebration, here a street party for children in Hull. Note the splendid aspidistra decorating the left-hand end of the table.

Raising the Maypole at Slingsby, near Malton, 1905. The late-Victorian interest in folk customs and heritage led to an enthusiastic revival of such traditions as dancing round the maypole. The village of Slingsby was noted for its lofty maypole, 90 ft high. This photograph is dated 15 May, so it was not being raised for the May Day celebrations themselves. The booth on the left suggests that perhaps it was being put in place for some local fair or village festivity.

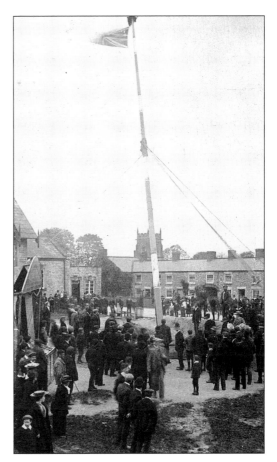

This is not a May Day event either. The girls were dancing at a Missionary Festival held at Ebberston Vicarage on 13 August 1914. The costumes of the older girls indicate that they were pupils at Ebberston Hall School. The date is rather poignant: nine days earlier, the British government had declared war on Germany.

No excuse for being unaware that Bostock and Wombwell's Circus had arrived in town after this impressive entry along Prospect Road into Scarborough in 1912. Children gazed 'awe-struck at the furrowed sides of the slate-grey monsters as they slowly pad their way along the street. . . . They go lurching past, turn the corner and disappear, with the excited but respectful knot of children following close behind.' (An interesting detail of the photograph is the tall, red and white striped barber's pole projecting from the wall on the left.)

'Success to Our Carnival' declares the banner stretching over a gaily decorated Clara Street, Pudsey, in 1905. The hospital cot in the centre suggests a fund-raising event for the local hospital, as does the stiff figure in a nurse's costume to the left of it. In fact, 'she' is a dummy which was brought out for each year's carnival.

Still only half its final height, the bonfire on Beacon Hill, near Pickering, constructed for King George V's Silver Jubilee celebrations on 6 May, 1935. On the right a farmer waits with another wagon-load of brushwood to add to the impressive pile.

At St James' Green, Thirsk, the same event was commemorated by a street party for local children. Each child was presented with one of the royal souvenir mugs which can be seen along the table and many of which are still treasured mementoes of the occasion. Almost as striking in its way is the sturdy tea urn. Heated by charcoal in the lower compartment, it could no doubt be relied on to provide a well-stewed cup of tea.

Withernsea was one of the most successful venues for Will Catlin's Pierrots. From his base at Scarborough Catlin managed several troupes of pierrots performing at seaside resorts along the east and south coast. Originally, the performances took place on the beach, but when the council raised their charges, Catlin moved his shows into local halls. During the winter the pierrot groups toured the inland towns.

This group, also at Withernsea, has obviously decided to stay in their makeshift theatre on the beach where a young lady from *The Merry Mascots* is giving a spirited rendition of a popular song. Seats cost 6*d*, standing room, 3*d*. Other groups which visited the Yorkshire resorts included *The Jovial Jollies*, *The Gay Cadets* and *The Smart Set Entertainers*.

At Butlin's Holiday Camp at Filey in the
1950s eighteen-year-old Diane
Hickingsbotham, 'a Clerk' from Ilkeston in
Derbyshire, is congratulated as the winner of
the Bathing Beauty Queen Contest. Mr (later
Sir) Billy Butlin, on the right, had opened his
first camp at Skegness in 1936 with the slogan
'A Week's Holiday for a Week's Pay' – then
about £3.50. The venture was a great success,
a second camp followed at Clacton and Filey
was the third. The individual chalets, all with
hot and cold water, and the non-stop
entertainment proved infinitely more
attractive than the dour boarding-houses
which up until then had dominated the low-
cost holiday market.

Part of the Butlin's camp at Filey. The Second World War, which began shortly after Butlin opened his
camp here, proved a blessing in disguise. The government bought his camps for army barracks,
appointed him Director-General of Hostels to the Ministry of Supply and at the end of the war sold the
camps back to him at a knock-down price. By 1947, in the depths of the austerity years, more than half
a million holiday-makers were flocking to his resorts. On arrival they handed in their ration books so
that their food coupons could be used to stock the kitchens.

The Kiddies Corner at Butlin's, Filey. This innovation was enormously popular with parents, leaving them free to sample the resort's other attractions, one of which was Britain's longest bar – 198 ft in length with twenty pumps spaced along it. Along with the rest of Britain's holiday industry, Butlin's suffered badly from the advent of cheap holidays in the sun. Filey camp was closed in 1984 and the site is now occupied as a caravan park.

This appears to be another Peace Day pageant, with the children costumed to suggest various First World War rôles. There is even a German officer there – the little boy sitting near the centre of the front row wearing a rather impressive helmet. The location of this colourful event is unknown.

HERITAGE,
TRADITION & PEOPLE

Amidst the luxuriant foliage of the Conservatory at Old Sleningford Hall, Mickley, near Ripon, two distinguished ladies (surely a little over-dressed for such a humid environment) enjoy one of Edwardian England's most rigorously observed traditions, afternoon tea. Their tea-table is a marvel of small-scale functional engineering. At the lower level is a rack of three plate-holders, the centre one bearing a substantial-looking fruit cake. On the upper part the gleaming teapot is suspended from a hoop so that it can be tipped, with the minimum of effort, to fill each cup.

It's a rare family nowadays that sits down formally at 4 o'clock for afternoon tea, one of those leisurely British rituals, like having a 'proper' breakfast, that faded away in the postwar years. But as the Heritage Industry gathers ever greater momentum these are small losses, amply replaced surely by repackaging whole swathes of the country under such titles as 'Catherine Cookson Country'. In the North Riding alone we have 'Herriot Country', 'Heartbeat Country' and 'Last of the Summer Wine Country'.

The photographs in this chapter illustrate a rather more varied pattern of heritage. The annual procession of the Ancient Order of Shepherds in Rosedale was a genuine tradition, as was the baking of the Great Denby Dale Pie (p. 109) and the sounding of the Watchman's horn at Ripon (p. 120), the last faithfully observed for more than a thousand years and still going strong.

Then there are the monuments, a form of commemoration generally out of favour nowadays, but providing across Yorkshire an attractive architectural focus in many a city square or country market place. For some reason the county had a definite liking for obelisks. The oldest one to have survived in Britain was set up in 1701 in Ripon Market Place. Designed by the architect Nicholas Hawksmoor, it still adds drama and elegance to the heart of the city. Many other obelisks followed, the most prominent of them the 60 ft

memorial to Captain Cook that stands high on the Cleveland Hills overlooking his childhood home at Great Ayton.

Heritage depends as much on people as on monuments, so I have included a few characters whom publishers thought famous or notorious enough to make printing postcards of them a commercial proposition. They range from the Sherburn gamekeeper, Tom Atkinson, famous for being murdered, to Miss Rose Carr of Hornsea, who fascinated her contemporaries by her extraordinary strength, by her hell-fire preaching and by the niggling doubts over her true gender.

More famous still were the residents of perhaps the most photographed home in the county, Haworth Parsonage (p. 117), at one time described as 'on the edge of the West Yorkshire Moors', nowadays as being 'in Brontë Country'. The story of the three gifted sisters who lived in this sturdy old Georgian building has captured public imagination almost as powerfully as the stirring, passionate novels they wrote there. Arts of a different kind are briefly represented here, perhaps most strikingly by the photograph of Leyburn's first 'Cinema House' (p. 117). Opened in 1915, this flimsy structure only lasted a year.

Also included in this chapter are some 'mysteries', photographs which are visually interesting but whose subjects are quite unfathomable, at least to me. Any help in unravelling these riddles would be most welcome.

The Ancient Order of Shepherds was one of many such friendly societies that flourished in Yorkshire during the latter part of the nineteenth century. Each year the members donned their sashes, decorated their shepherds' crooks with flowers and paraded through the village for a church service followed by a dinner. At Lealholm they built their own club room, a men-only refuge with rules modelled on the famous London clubs. The building is still there, now a restaurant and tea room.

The special dish constructed for the Great Denby Dale Pie of 1928 is revealed to the world. The first of these huge pies was baked in 1788 to celebrate George III's return to sanity: later ones marked the victory of Waterloo and Queen Victoria's Jubilees. The 1928 monster meal was organized to raise £1,000 for the Huddersfield Royal Infirmary but the festivities were almost cancelled when the organizers discovered that a large part of the pie had gone bad. Four barrowloads of stinking meat were secretly spirited away, a fact that has only recently been revealed. Perhaps because of that mishap, no more great pies were attempted until 1964 when it was decided to commemorate the four royal births of that year. On this occasion two walls of Mr Hector Buckley's barn, in which the pie had been baked, had to be demolished to get it out.

Children gather around the memorial to the famous geologist Adam Sedgwick in Dent. Sedgwick was born in this remote village near the Cumbrian border, where his father was vicar, in 1785. The study of geology at that time was primarily an occupation for amateurs, but Sedgwick brought an academic discipline to the examination of rock formations. His geological studies broke new ground in describing and explaining such complex areas as the Pennine hills and the Devonian system of south-west England. Ingeniously contained within the large block of Shap granite that forms his monument is a fountain.

The soaring monument to William Wilberforce, erected in 1834, provides a dramatic focus for Hull's city centre. The 'Great Liberator' was born here in 1759 and became MP for Hull at the age of twenty-one, following an election in which his success was ensured by spending the colossal sum of £70,000 in bribing the voters. His twenty-year campaign for the withdrawal of Britain from the slave trade culminated in the historic Anti-Slavery Act of 1807. The Wilberforce family home in the old High Street is now a museum dedicated to his memory and to the history of slavery.

'Erected by his tenantry and friends' in 1871, this exuberantly Gothic monument to the 2nd Earl of Feversham is still the most striking feature of the Market Square in Helmsley. 'Tenantry and friends' must have genuinely wanted to honour the late Earl since they engaged no less an architect than Sir George Gilbert Scott to design the memorial tower. Scott was famous for his Albert Memorial in London and although this monument (in what was then a remote part of Yorkshire) is on a much smaller scale, it is just as lavish in its abundance of architectural decoration.

I find this photographic portrait of the 3rd Earl of Feversham and his grandchild quite extraordinary. Unlike the subjects of most photographic portraits taken in the late 1890s, the smiling child and his fine-featured grandfather both seem completely at ease with the camera. Technically it is an impeccable example of the photographer's art, and whoever took this photograph must also have established a quite unusual rapport with both the Earl and his grandchild. I wish I knew the photographer's name.

For some reason Yorkshire towns and cities seem to have had a fondness for setting up obelisks. Like this one in Richmond Market Place, they were usually surmounted by a cross and so known as Market Crosses. The first obelisk on this site was raised in 1471, possibly to mark the town's underground reservoir holding 12,000 gallons over which it stood. This obelisk was 'removed for some unaccountable reason' exactly 300 years later and replaced by the present structure. This postcard view, taken around 1908, was produced by the Local View Emporium of High Row, Richmond.

Ripon's 90 ft high obelisk, also known as the Market Cross, is the oldest one surviving in England, designed by the famous architect Nicholas Hawksmoor and erected in 1701. Eighty years later it was in need of repair. As a plaque on the obelisk says, the work was carried out 'at the expense of William Aislabie, Esquire, who represented this borough in Parliament sixty years'. The City Fathers were clearly carried away by their gratitude for Mr Aislabie's munificence since the plaque credits him not just with repairing the monument but with having erected it in the first place.

This obelisk in Huddersfield Road, Barnsley, was erected in 1866 following a pit disaster. The design includes a bronze angel carrying a wounded man – several of the victims were members of rescue parties who were killed when further explosions blasted through the mine. There are other Yorkshire obelisks at Harrogate (the war memorial), in the village of Osmotherley, near Northallerton, in the grounds of Castle Howard, near Malton, and, most prominent of all, the Captain Cook monument high on the Cleveland Hills.

The tradition that links Robin Hood with this dramatic stretch of the coast south of Whitby is, alas, completely spurious. That has not stopped generations of visitors coming to the picturesque village where the houses seem to be built on top of one another, at one time providing an impenetrable refuge for smugglers. The novelist Leo Walmsley lived at Robin Hood's Bay and used it as the model for the fishing-village of 'Bramblewick'.

The photographs on these two pages are all mysterious to me. I came across this portrait of an obviously well-to-do family, in their Sunday best by the look of it, in a box of old books about Yorkshire. Someone has written 'Bedale Hall' on the back but the porch shown here is certainly not part of that grand old house.

This commercial postcard is identified simply as 'Cleckheaton' (near Bradford). But what is the strange ceremony that appears to be in progress? The man second from left is showing the toddler some foliage while the man in the light-coloured suit in the centre clearly thinks that the moment is of some significance since he is taking a photograph of it. What on earth is going on?

This picture is also from a postcard published by a commercial photographer in Batley. The headwear suggests a date in the late 1920s: it is much more difficult to imagine what this merry party was celebrating or to assess the significance of the naked, hairless doll cradled by the smiling lady on the left.

This unusual postcard was published by a Withernsea firm in 1911. Its caption, 'The Busy Bees', is taken from the chalked inscription on the spade held by the man in the centre of the picture. But who were they? Estate workers, possibly, proudly displaying the tools of their trade.

The Arts in Yorkshire. Amateur artists sketching at Beauchief Abbey, near Sheffield, *c.* 1912. The fourteenth-century tower is all that remains of the medieval abbey: the rest, already in ruins, was cannibalized by Edward Pegge in the 1670s to build his great house nearby.

An art class at Northallerton Grammar School in the early 1950s. The pupils have been presented with a superb collection of stuffed animals to work from, including, in the top right-hand corner of the picture, a fearsome head of a gorilla.

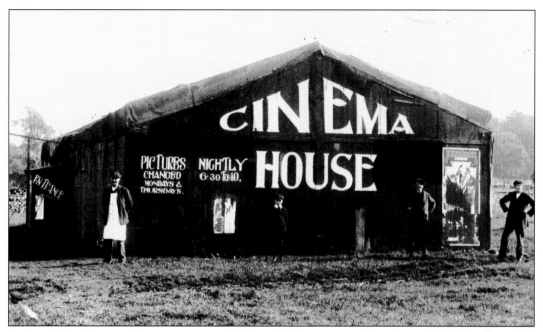

Leyburn's first Cinema House, erected in 1915 in a field between the Harmby and Middleham roads. It offers a generous 3½ hours of entertainment, from 6.30 to 10 p.m., with 'Pictures changed Mondays and Thursdays'. The tattered poster on the right is advertising the productions of the Keystone Company, renowned for its 'Keystone Cops' comedy films. This cinema lasted little over a year, being pulled down in 1916. A new cinema, the Elite, was built closer to the Market Place and this survived until the early 1970s. Miraculously, it reopened in 1994 and is currently the only cinema in the Dales.

'Haworth Parsonage in the time of the Brontës' says the caption on this immensely popular postcard. The claim seems highly dubious since Charlotte, the last of the Brontë sisters, died in 1855. At that time camera technology was still fairly primitive and even the most gifted photographer would have been lucky to produce a picture as technically excellent as this. It is much more likely that an enterprising commercial photographer, probably in the 1890s, staged the scene with actors in the hope of capitalizing on the steady stream of tourists already making their way to this literary shrine.

Tommy Dick, newsvendor in the Greenside area of Pudsey, photographed in 1920. From his wooden hut he sold copies of the *Sporting Pink*, the *Green Post* and the paper he is displaying here, the *Bramley and District Weekly Advertiser*.

Anna Strickland, seated in the centre of this picture with her granddaughter Annie Florence, was well known in the Rosedale hamlet of Thorgill. Born in 1823, she married William Strickland and together they had twelve children, ten of whom survived. According to a family story, as a young bride Anna planted a random selection of seeds in this garden among which was the monkey-puzzle tree, just visible in the background. At the age of eighty and in poor health, Anna was taken by the fancy of having her coffin made from its timber. The tree was felled and the coffin constructed. However, it was another nine years before it was required. Her coffin was then carried to Lastingham churchyard by four bearers whom she herself had named and for whom she had left four half-crowns (12½p) on the mantelpiece of her parlour.

The night of Friday 11 November 1904 was snowy and moonlit. About 10 o'clock a group of gamekeepers on an estate near Sherburn came across a gang of poachers. In the 'desperate and fatal affray' that followed, gamekeeper Tom Atkinson was shot and later died and two others were seriously wounded. Three of the poachers were caught and convicted of manslaughter. Two brothers, Charles and William (Curly Bill) Hovington, were sentenced to ten years imprisonment; their accomplice, Thomas 'Fez' Dobson received a seven-year term.

As a young woman Miss Rose Carr of Hornsea was famed for her thrilling performances as a fire and brimstone preacher. She earned her living as a carrier and apparently thought nothing of carrying two 16 stone sacks of grain, one under each arm, up the steps to the granary. Her massive build, fiery temperament, deep husky voice and spinster status all fanned the rumours that she was really a man. Rose died at the age of seventy in 1913 but the mystery of her sex remained unresolved even then, since she was laid out by her sister.

Tom Hawley, the Ripon Hornblower, who held the office from 1941 to 1955. The sounding of three blasts of the horn at 9 p.m. every night in Ripon's Market Square is one of the most venerable of Yorkshire traditions, going back at least a thousand years. The original horn dating from 886 can still be seen in the Town Hall. From the time the horn was sounded until 3 or 4 o'clock the next morning, the Wakeman, or Watchman, was personally and financially responsible for the security of the city's houses and property. In return householders in Elizabethan times paid the watchman 4*d* (1.6p) a year if their house had two or more doors, 2*d* a year if they had only one. The 9 p.m. timing of the horn-blowing has remained constant over the centuries apart from a short period just before the First World War when a tourist-conscious City Council decided to vary it slightly 'so that visitors from Harrogate could witness the ceremony and still catch the 9.29 p.m. train'.

REST & RECREATION

One of the spectacular events at the Grand York Gala. Established in 1859, the Gala was a three-day event offering sports contests and the traditional fun of the fair. It flourished right up until 1914.

Any true Yorkshireman will know them off by heart, but here are a few statistics about cricket in the county during this half-century. The highest batting score in a Test Match, 364, was knocked up by Len Hutton (born in Pudsey) against Australia in 1938. The largest crowd ever gathered in England to watch a cricket match was 46,000 for the match against Lancashire at Old Trafford on 2 August 1926. Yorkshire won the County Championship more often than any other county, twenty-nine times in all. At a less exalted level, few towns or even villages failed to muster their own teams for Saturday afternoon matches.

Cricket may have been the county's main obsession, but cycling was also enormously popular. Richmond cyclists formed the first Bicycle Touring Club in the world, in 1878, and their annual 'Bicycle Meets' brought many hundreds of cyclists to the town. Tennis as an outdoor game appeared around the same time and quickly supplanted croquet and badminton as the middle-class 'recreation of choice'. For those in search of more dangerous sport, there were motor-cycle and car scrambles, most famously at Rosedale Bank where drivers faced the daunting challenge of a gradient of 1 in $2\frac{1}{2}$, the steepest in Britain.

There were infinite opportunities for more leisurely pursuits. A gentle stroll through the wild gardens at Hackfall near Ripon, perhaps, pausing to wonder at the curious follies set up there in the 1750s (p. 134). Country people would clamber into dusty farm wagons drawn by beflowered and beribboned horses for excursions to local beauty spots or the nearest seaside resort. Later they travelled in slightly more comfort in open charabancs. For the small number affluent enough to own an automobile, the country roads were virtually empty (though in a shocking state) and the first motoring guides to Yorkshire's many attractions appeared in the early 1900s.

Even if you couldn't get away from the city, you could still take advantage of the many public parks that had been lovingly created by Victorian and Edwardian municipal councils as an expression of civic pride. Park-keepers ensured that no unseemly behaviour took place, and a tribe of gardeners guaranteed a dazzling display of flowers. As part of a friendly rivalry between the various parks, gardeners vied with one another in producing ever more elaborate constructions like the floral Grand Piano that formed a centrepiece of the display in Bradford's Bowling Park in 1923 (p. 129).

Tennis partners at Barmby on the Moor. The game in its present form suddenly took off in the 1870s and became immensely popular in middle-class society as a decorous form of sport in which both men and women could take part. The rules of the game have scarcely changed since they were formulated in 1877 by the All-England Lawn Tennis and Croquet Club in preparation for the first Wimbledon tournament in that year. A slightly earlier form of the game, played on a court shaped like an hourglass, found little favour.

It was in Richmond that the first Bicycle Touring Club in the world was formed on 5 August 1878 and five years later became the Cyclists' Touring Club. The sport became even more popular after the invention of the pneumatic tyre in 1888 by John Dunlop. The virtual absence of motor traffic made these the golden years of cycling. Hundreds of clubs were established across the county and were particularly active in the West Riding. When not on the move, cycling clubs loved organizing contests for the best-decorated bicycle, often combined with a fancy dress competition, like this one in the Ripon area.

Two smartly decorated horses drawing a full wagon-load of villagers prepare to set off from Kilham, probably for a day out at Bridlington, 7 miles away. Flowers have been threaded around the horses' headbands, forehead and nosebands, as well as on the hames (the curved parts) of the collar; ribbons have been tied around their necks. Summer excursions like this would set off around 6 a.m. and not return until about 9 p.m.

This looks very much like an Economy Class excursion with only a precarious bench set up along the centre of the trailer. The photograph was taken in the Market Place, Pickering, by the town's distinguished photographer Sydney Smith (1884–1958), *c.* 1919.

A newspaper poll in 1907 voted Thornton le Dale 'Yorkshire's Prettiest Village'. With Thornton Beck rippling alongside its quiet main street, the picturesque old cross and stocks and open country all around, the accolade was well deserved, although one can think of scores of other Yorkshire villages which might make an equal claim to the title. The impressive vintage car parked on the left is interesting, its chauffeur apparently concerned with some mechanical problem, perhaps the front offside wheel which seems to be skewed at a curious angle. The car's number-plate, SN 20, reveals that this was only the twentieth car to be registered in Dundee. So these are Scottish tourists, harbingers of the late twentieth-century tide of visitors who have turned the quiet country road on which they have parked into the ceaselessly busy A170.

For their chapel choir outing in the 1920s this Huddersfield party engaged a splendid open-top charabanc. For once most of the names have been recorded. On the top deck (6th and 7th from left) are John and Hilda Taylor who ran the Central Stores at Deighton. The man holding a trilby (4th from right) is Arthur Nunns Priestley, the choirmaster.

Farndale Daffodils

'Daffodils that come before the swallow dares, and take the winds of March with beauty.' The daffodils that stretch for 6 miles along the banks of the River Dove in early spring have been attracting visitors to Farndale since early Victorian times. Growing wild, the daffodils are short-stemmed, their colours varying from a pale buttercup yellow to a rich orange-gold. Local tradition asserts that the bulbs were cultivated by monks from the nearby abbeys who used the petals in medical concoctions. For generations visitors plucked a few blooms to take home but by the late 1940s some half a million were being collected. The site is now protected by the Nature Conservancy Council, but visitors are still welcome.

Reservoir and Bridge, Gouthwaite, Pateley Bridge

The huge reservoir at Gouthwaite, above Pateley Bridge, drowned 2 miles of Nidderdale. Today, such a violation of the environment would be highly contentious. When it was built in the 1860s, however, the reservoir with an embankment, 180 ft high and 500 ft long, was acclaimed as 'one of the finest engineering feats in Yorkshire'. Excursion parties and private motorists like this one followed the narrow lanes up the dale to view this inland lake.

These stepping stones at Bolton Woods on the River Wharfe north of Ilkley provided a charming setting for picnics. This postcard was sent towards the end of the First World War and the writer asks to be excused for not replying earlier 'but my sweetheart returned from France just when your flowers came & we've been so taken up I've never managed time to write anyone. . . . Harry returns on Monday to France'.

An appealing holiday scene at a cove on Filey Bay which stretches some 6 miles from Filey Brigg to Bempton Cliffs. Filey became a favoured seaside resort in the early 1800s, a popularity boosted by the arrival of the railway in 1847. The little town was regarded as a gentler alternative to the sophisticated attractions of Scarborough, 7 miles to the north, and it still retains considerable period charm and flavour.

One of the most attractive traits of our Victorian and Edwardian forefathers was their passion for creating public parks. Woodhouse Moor was the Hyde Park of Leeds and had been laid out in walks and avenues as early as the 1850s with an area to the east left as wild moorland. On summer Sundays as many as eight or ten thousand people might be strolling here as a brass band played sacred music. This area was known as the 'Parliament', a jocular reference to the knots of men who gathered here and discussed the issues of the day.

Peasholm Park, Scarborough, in the 1920s. Municipally owned, the park offered a huge variety of entertainment. There were brass band concerts with musicians playing from the floating bandstand (on the left), a Chinese pagoda and waterfall, beautifully maintained gardens and, perhaps most popular of all, the unique sea battles fought with miniature craft. These naval warfare displays are still a regular part of the park's summer entertainment programme.

A colourful corner of Sherwood's Gardens, Hornsea, with a life-size statue of a kilted Scotsman. The gardens were later known as Tansley Gardens after their new owner. Mr Tansley was a greengrocer and part of the stock for his shop came from vegetable patches interspersed among the floral displays here.

Park gardeners strove to out-do each other in creating the most intricate and impressive floral effects. This striking production appeared in Bradford's Bowling Park in 1923.

The towers of York Minster rise in the background of this photograph recording the members of the North Eastern Railway's District Engineer's Office Tennis Club in 1921. Their tennis wear is considerably more practical than that worn by the couple on p. 123.

PADDLING POOL, WHARFE MEADOWS PARK, OTLEY.

The paddling pool in Wharfe Meadows Park, Otley, in 1928. The land for the park was given to Otley Urban Council in 1924 by Major Fawkes of Farnley Hall. The completed park included a sandpit, see-saws and swings for the children; for grown-ups there were open-air baths, tennis courts, a 9-hole putting course, a bowling green and boating on the River Wharfe which runs alongside the park.

An early Frazer Nash sports car attempts the Rosedale hillclimb, *c.* 1924. Rosedale Chimney presented a serious challenge since it was the steepest public road in Britain with a gradient of 1 in 2½. Spectator safety at these popular events was blithely disregarded until a bystander was killed in March 1925. Captain Frazer Nash founded his company in 1924 and during its early years it did well, but with the advance of mass production models it was forced to close in 1957.

Motor Hill Climb Roll,
sedale Abbey. June 1914.

The same location, ten years earlier, in June 1914. The motor-cycle looks like the famous Indian V-twin model, introduced earlier that year. Well designed and sturdily constructed, the 'Indians' incorporated such advanced features as rear suspension, twist-grip controls and electric lighting. In essentials modern motor-cycles have made few improvements on this extremely successful model.

Bishop Wilton is a picturesque village on the edge of the Wolds where medieval Archbishops of York had one of their palaces. That has disappeared entirely and the village is best known nowadays for its dedication to cricket. In 1927 the villagers formed a team all of whose members were over seventy years old and issued an open challenge to any other team of similarly mature years. Here the captain 'Joby' Johnson (second from right) and wicket-keeper Mr Ware lead the team onto the field for a match against Sheepshed at Huddersfield.

'Joby' Johnson, straight from his innings, enjoys a pint. In view of their advanced years, batsmen were excused running: markers around the field determined whether a hit should count as one, two or three runs. The first recorded match of the Bishop Wilton Cricket Club took place in August 1865 'with the Thixendale drum and fife band in attendance'. The club is still going strong – indeed in 1997 the team won the Independent League Cup. At this 1927 match, however, they lost to Sheepshed, and again when a return match was played at Bishop Wilton.

The captain of the Sheepshed team somewhat anxiously faces up to the Bishop Wilton bowling in front of a wicket formed by three walking sticks.

An Edwardian group of visitors at Mowbray Castle, Hackfall, near Ripon. The 'Castle' is not one of Yorkshire's many medieval relics but one of four follies created around 1750 by the celebrated architect William Aislabie (1700–81) in landscaped grounds where the River Ure flows through a narrow gorge. Hackfall quickly became a fixed point on the itinerary of eighteenth- and nineteenth-century visitors to the Vale of Mowbray. J.M.W. Turner came to the park in 1816, leaving behind an alluring watercolour of a sylvan scene; three views of the 'Castle' appear on the famous Wedgwood service designed for Catherine the Great, the only location to appear there more than once.

Hackfall was still flourishing when this Edwardian party paused outside another of the follies, but after the First World War the gardens became overgrown and the artificial ruins were in danger of turning into genuine ones. The Woodland Trust has now assumed responsibility for selective replanting of trees and the Hackfall Trust was created in 1987 with the aim of restoring the buildings. The steep, narrow paths however will not be upgraded to modern tourist expectations but maintained as far as possible just as they were in Hackfall's heyday.

MILES TO TRAVEL

An early motorist poses in her serviceable two-seater at Low Row in Swaledale. The vehicle had been registered at Newcastle in 1904 so this elderly lady, whose left eye has a distinctly glassy appearance, would not have had to take a driving test (they were not introduced until 1934), nor would she have paid a Road Fund Tax (first levied in 1909 at an annual charge of 2 guineas, £2.10). Another lady motorist, Mrs Rodolph Stawell, author of *Motor Tours in Yorkshire*, published in 1909, travelled along this very road which she described as 'not very good, and there are some steep pitches between Gunnerside and Reeth; but it matters little, for who would care to hurry through such a land as this?'

'Thank God for lanes wherein no traffic whirls / In deadly line . . . / Here may the harassed spirit find relief / From rush and blare.' This is not John Betjeman on his favourite hobby-horse but the less well-known John Merrick, writing about Yorkshire in the 1750s. A century and a half later Arthur H. Norway, walking along the Great North Road, reflected on 'its deserted ways'. 'Only cyclists and ragged beggarmen' or 'yonder sleepy farmer jogging home from Doncaster in his gig' disturbed the peace of the 'broad old highway running straight and smooth between wide grassy borders'.

Arthur Norway walked for pleasure as did the Revd A.N. Cooper (p. 147), the author of such popular walking guides as *With Knapsack and Notebook*. But for most country people at the turn of the century, walking was a matter of necessity, while in the towns 'walking fever' manifested itself in races like the one shown here at Hull (p. 146).

Railways meanwhile were enjoying a golden age with a vast network, frequent services and inexpensive fares. Even the small communities along the length of Wensleydale enjoyed their own railway which provided a link between the main East Coast route at Northallerton and the Settle & Carlisle railway at Garsdale Head. As J.S. Fletcher wrote in 1914 of the dalesmen, 'Their grandparents were born into a world of unconquerable distance – they themselves live next door to everywhere'. In the North York Moors some of the most remote villages and hamlets of the county were served by the Pickering to Whitby line, a route which was a victim of the Beeching cuts; part of it now prospers as the privately owned North York Moors Railway.

Yorkshire's rivers and canals in 1900 were still crowded with colliers and barges, although they were steadily losing ground against road traffic. By the time the canals were nationalized in 1962 almost half the network had closed. The triumph of the motor vehicle as the predominant twentieth-century form of private and commercial transport brought huge economic benefits, opened up parts of the county's spectacular scenery to millions and at the same time altered for ever the character of our towns, cities and countryside.

Little more than a novelty in the early 1900s, the aeroplane was also to transform people's lives during this half-century. Before the First World War aerobatic displays delighted the crowds on Scarborough beach (p. 144); during the war they played a fairly small rôle, mainly in reconnaissance. The interwar years saw a slow but steady growth in passenger traffic, and in the Second World War the aeroplane became the deliverer of destruction on a scale inconceivable until then. The half-century ended with the arrival of the first jet plane, the *Comet*, in 1951, ushering in the age of mass transportation by air.

Rush hour on the Great North Road at Doncaster, *c.* 1912. A decade earlier Arthur H. Norway, on a walking tour in the area, contrasted the coaching days on the Great North Road, 'so full of noisy life', with its 'now deserted ways'. Note the contemporary equivalent of a Little Chef on the left offering mineral water for sale and the solitary petrol pump on the right.

Construction work almost completed on the by-pass at Sinnington, near Pickering, in 1936. A rope attached to a beer barrel cordons off the new road, in the distance a steam-roller is at work on the surface and the large board gives the stern admonition, 'STEADY PLEASE'. The by-pass straightened out a kink in the main Thirsk to Scarborough road, the A170, and has not been substantially improved since then.

The Great North Road at Scotch Corner near Richmond in the 1940s. This is now a major interchange on the A1, already a four-lane dual carriageway with plans in place to upgrade it to full motorway standard. Scotch Corner was given its name because travellers had the choice here of continuing along the Great North Road to the east coast of Scotland or bearing left on the A66 (running towards the top of the picture) to Penrith, Carlisle and the west coast. The Scotch Corner Hotel is still here: it too has recently been upgraded and refurbished.

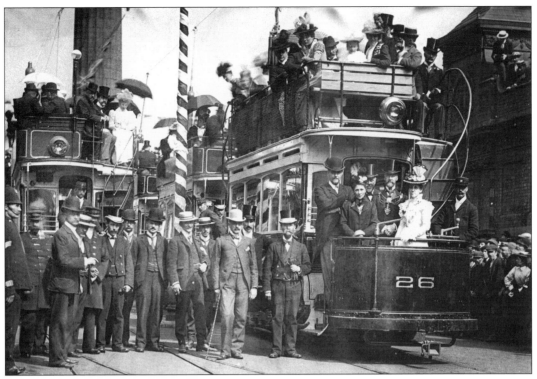

An impressive group of city notables, led by the Mayor, Alderman Larard, gather at the depot to inaugurate Hull's first tram service in 1899. During the first six months of operation more than 4 million passengers travelled on these stately vehicles.

A dramatic scene at Dewsbury in 1915 when a Dewsbury Ossett tram careered down the hill and embedded itself in the Scarbro Hotel, just off the Market Place. It was on its way to the terminus lower down the hill. Surprisingly no one was injured. According to some Yorkshire tram enthusiasts the word tram derives from a Sheffield man, James Outram, who as an engineer at the Duke of Norfolk's colliery there first conceived this form of road transport.

Whitby railway station on 1 June 1936. The Esk Valley line from Middlesbrough to Whitby is one of the most scenic routes in the country but, when this photograph was taken, the route was already under threat with just three trains on Sundays, six on weekdays and nine on Saturdays. Miraculously the line escaped the Beeching cuts and, despite continual mutterings from British Rail, is still in operation although nowadays only a single track leads into the station. At Grosmont the Esk Valley connects with that great railway revival, the North York Moors Railway.

A passenger/goods train approaches Levisham station, *c.* 1938. This dramatic route through Newtondale was originally engineered by George Stephenson in 1836 and follows the course of a glacial overflow channel. In the early years the service consisted of a 40-seater coach hauled by a single horse, which was assisted at steeper sections by a second. The line was axed by Beeching in 1965 but railway enthusiasts rallied around and the Pickering to Grosmont railway, renamed the North York Moors Railway, re-opened as a private company on 2 February 1969. A journey along the 18-mile route is now an essential experience for visitors to this north-eastern corner of the county.

A motley group of desperate-looking men monopolize a bench outside the Kingston Street building of the Manchester, Sheffield & Lincolnshire Railway in Hull. The railway's initials, MSL, were popularly interpreted as standing for 'Mucky, Slow and Lazy'. Its outpost at Hull, opened in 1879, did not provide passenger services but was a freight depot from which a 1¾-mile branch line joined the main NER line along which the MSL trains travelled to join their own network at Selby. The MSL later changed its name to the Grand Central Railway.

This splendid locomotive headed the first train on the Askrigg to Hawes section of the Wensleydale Railway opened on 1 June 1878. It is seen here at Leyburn Station, *c.* 1898. Passenger traffic along the dale was never very heavy – even at its peak in 1919 Leyburn was only issuing an average of 100 or so tickets a day. That figure steadily declined and the last passenger train covered the route on 24 April 1954. On board was Mr Christopher Jones of Hawes who could claim that he had seen the first train on the line and travelled on the last. Freight services to the limestone quarries at Redmire continued until the 1980s and currently the Wensleydale Railway Association is campaigning energetically for the restoration of passenger services along the dale. (Note for trainspotters: the engine is a Fletcher BTP 0–4–4 tank engine, No. 588, built at Gateshead in 1877.)

Barges on the River Hull in the 1930s. Commercial traffic on Britain's canals and rivers was still important, with more than 19 million tonnes of cargo being transported every year. The River Hull flows into the Humber estuary and merchants were trading at the point where the rivers meet in Norman times. By 1203 the port ranked sixth in the country, exporting wool to Flanders and importing French wine to England. After a long decline throughout most of this century recent substantial investment has now made Kingston upon Hull the fastest-growing port in the country.

The Harbour at Bedale, *c.* 1909. Bedale is about as land-locked as you can get, with the nearest seaboard more than 50 miles distant. The 'harbour' is in fact a canal basin and was built during the canal-building frenzy of the late 1700s. The idea was to convert the tiny Bedale Beck into a 6-mile long canal to join the River Swale at Morton. Construction began in 1768 but shortly after this basin was completed funds ran out and the project was abandoned. The great iron mooring rings installed then are still in place.

Barges on the Sheffield and South Yorkshire Navigation at Doncaster in 1913 with St George's Church in the background. At that time, it was possible to travel continuously by canal and river from Doncaster to places as far apart as Liverpool, Bristol and Guildford, a total of nearly 3,900 navigable miles in all. By the time British Waterways took over the network in 1962 only 2,000 miles were still passable.

Bentfield C. Hucks flying upside down over Scarborough in 1914. Such aerobatic demonstrations were immensely popular in the years before the First World War and B.C. Hucks enjoyed a national reputation as a competition flyer and test pilot. He was the first pilot to fly upside down and the first to loop the loop. Throughout the war he continued as Chief Test Pilot, his daredevil career coming to a singularly inappropriate end only when he succumbed to the Spanish 'flu epidemic that took some 225,000 lives in the winter of 1918/19.

An unusual photograph, taken from the R100 airship which was built at Hedon in 1929. These quiet, spacious Leviathans of the sky were highly popular with travellers in the 1920s and '30s despite the crash of the R100's sister ship, the R101, in 1930 when forty-eight people were killed. But when the *Hindenburg*, the world's largest airship, came down in flames in 1937, the brief age of the airship was over.

Amy Johnson, 'The Wonder Airwoman', was born in Hull in 1903, gained her pilot's licence in 1929 and in the following year became the first woman to fly solo to Australia. She made a record-breaking solo flight to Cape Town in 4½ days, taking 'a few books, maps, a bag full of iron rations and a pith helmet'. Hull's Rotary Club laid on a splendid presentation for her at which an 'immortal anthem' was sung, the last verse of which goes: 'How d'ye do, Amy Johnson, how d'ye do? / From Croydon to Australia you flew, / And we were so glad to see / That His Gracious Majesty / Honoured you with CBE. How d'ye do?' At the outbreak of the Second World War Amy joined the Air Transport Auxiliary as a pilot, but on 5 January 1941 was lost after baling out over the Thames Estuary.

For most Edwardians 'taking the cure' at Harrogate, walking was an integral part of the treatment. The day began with an early morning visit to the Old Sulphur Well to swallow as best they could a glass of the disgusting water. During the remaining hours one surveyed the many shops, dallied as long as possible over one's tea or coffee, listened to the band in the Valley Gardens or took the air by means of a gentle stroll either on the 200 acres of the town's sacrosanct open grassland, the Stray, or on the even more expansive spaces of the surrounding moors, as here at Harlow Moor.

In 1903 a Hull newspaper deplored the 'walking fever' that had gripped the nation. The writer mocked the 'grotesque style' of some of the competitors in walking races. Perhaps he had just witnessed this contest, organized by Hull grocers. Recreational walks of 20 or 30 miles were routine; country children took a daily 5-mile walk to school in their stride.

The Revd A.N. Cooper, 'The Walking Parson', about to set off on one of his prodigious walks, fully equipped with umbrella, knapsack and stout boots which he had softened by pouring whiskey into them. The Revd Mr Cooper was vicar of Filey for a record-breaking fifty-five years, from 1880 to 1935, but acquired a much wider reputation as the author of books describing his walks across the length and breadth of Yorkshire: *Across the Broad Acres*, *With Knapsack and Notebook* and *The Tramps of the Walking Parson* were just three of his best-selling volumes. Born a southerner, he described himself as 'something like the typical Yorkshireman of literature – big of body, red-faced and hearty'. He was fond of telling the many people he met on his walks that his parish was unique: the town of Filey was located in the East Riding, its church and graveyard lay just over the boundary inside the North Riding. The Revd Cooper died in 1943 at the age of ninety-three.

'The End of a long trail' says the caption on this photograph of a group of young men on South Bay Sands at Scarborough. Early that summer morning in 1937 they had left the village of Cropton, some 24 miles distant. For two or three hours they enjoyed the attractions of this popular resort and then they began the six- or seven-hour walk back home. Such marathon walking excursions were commonplace: this one has been recorded only because the man on the extreme left of the group is Raymond Hayes, a Pickering-based commercial photographer who captured on film almost every aspect of local life in and around Ryedale between the 1930s and 1960s.

Harry Fitton of Huddersfield on his twenty-first birthday in 1902 with his brand-new motor-cycle, believed to be the first seen in the city. These early cycles had no suspension and on all but the smoothest of roads the rider (and bike) were rattled to bits. 'The brakes were extremely inefficient. They were so under-powered that the bike was unable to climb anything more than a slight incline without having to pedal.'

In 1922 the number of car registrations in Britain passed the 1 million mark for the first time. Despite there being many fewer vehicles on the road, deaths from road accidents in the 1920s and '30s were astonishingly high, varying between 5,500 and 7,000 each year. Compare that with the 1990s, when the average was around 3,800. This pretty comprehensive write-off seems to be the result of the driver failing to negotiate the sharp bend in the road visible on the left. Shortly after this photograph was taken the Highway Code was published for the first time (1931).

Two dapper young men on a smart BSA motor-cycle and sidecar outside York Minster in the early 1920s. The card bearing the number '29', just behind the registration plate, suggests they are taking part in some kind of contest or one of the 'Treasure Trails' popular at the time. The number-plate itself indicates that the vehicle had been registered at Sligo in the Republic of Ireland.

A magnificent, state-of-the-art road-roller comes to grips with a city street in Hull.

I'm looking
out for you
at BARNSLEY

An irresistible invitation to visit Barnsley. As with the promotional card for Bridlington (p. 39), this charming lady also appeared on postcards advertising the attractions of towns and cities all round the country.

This view of Victoria Road around the turn of the century suggests that there were indeed some attractive areas in 'Black Barnsley', a name it had earned as early as 1727 when Daniel Defoe made a brief visit. The town, he said, 'was eminent still for the working in iron and steel; and indeed the very town looks as black and smoky as if they were all smiths that lived in it'. Victoria Road looks positively suburban in this photograph, but there is now an industrial estate just off to the left.

THE SECOND WORLD WAR & THE NEW ELIZABETHAN AGE

At Croft aerodrome, the full complement of 431 Squadron pose on, and in front of, their new Halifax Mk III on 18 April 1944. Wing Commander Newsam sits in the centre of the front row. Croft, just inside the North Riding border near Darlington, was one of seventeen operational airfields in Yorkshire. During the course of the war 840 of the aircraft that took off from these fields did not return; more than 5,000 airmen were lost, among them hundreds of pilots, whose average age was twenty years six months.

Between 1939 and 1945 the city of Hull suffered 82 bombing raids in which 1,200 people were killed and another 3,000 seriously injured. More than 87,000 houses were destroyed, leaving 152,000 homeless. Half the city centre was reduced to rubble along with major stretches of the dockland areas. It would take decades before the city fully recovered from this onslaught.

The people of the Dales and Moors escaped destruction of this kind, but as the war dragged on they, like everyone else in the country, suffered the privations of rationing, restrictions on travel and pettifogging directives from bureaucrats. At Ravenseat, for example, high in the hills in Upper Swaledale, the local farmers were amazed to receive an edict from Whitehall instructing them to help the war effort by growing corn. In late November they regretfully informed the government that they were still waiting for the corn to ripen.

The comparative safety of much of the county meant that many evacuees were sent here from the threatened areas of the south-east. All householders with space available were expected to put it at the disposal of the Billeting Officer. Thus it was that for several months the historic house of Ripley Castle, near Harrogate, was occupied by children from a Dr Barnardo's home (p. 153).

The war ended with the capitulation of Japan on 14 August 1945, only to be followed by the 'Age of Austerity', a decade and more during which shortages and rationing became far more severe than anything experienced during the war itself. The Royal Wedding of Princess Elizabeth and Prince Philip in 1947, the London Olympic Games of 1948 and the Festival of Britain in 1951 all provided some relief from the general drabness of life, but it was not until the Coronation of 1953 that the nation finally seemed to shake itself free of its postwar gloom.

The mood may have been changed by the Coronation but the economic realities of a nation bankrupted by the war effort had not. Another ten years would pass before the benefits of America's Marshall Aid and a worldwide trade boom would enable Prime Minister Macmillan to assure the British people, 'You've never had it so good!' But looking back it seems clear now that the turning-point was the day in June 1953 when millions of Britons, lining the streets of London or clustered around the tiny, yellowish screens of their television sets, rediscovered their confidence and optimism as a nation.

Children evacuated from a Dr Barnardo's Home in London enjoy a picnic in the stately surroundings of Ripley Castle, near Harrogate, in 1940. They were just a few of the 800,000 schoolchildren and more than half a million mothers with pre-school age babies and toddlers evacuated from London and other prime targets of the Luftwaffe to areas deemed safe from bombing raids. There anyone with a spare bedroom had to fill it. Affluent middle-class families in the safe shires suddenly found themselves playing reluctant hosts (for an allowance of 10*s* 6*d*, 52½p, a week per head) to children from the poorest parts of East London, a clash of cultures whose comic aspects were memorably exploited by Evelyn Waugh in his 1942 novel *Put Out More Flags*.

Ripley Castle is a lovely Tudor building completed in 1555 by Sir William Ingilby. His direct descendants, Sir Thomas Ingilby and family, live there today. During the 'phoney war' of late September to mid-1940, however, this historic house, like many others, was commandeered to provide a safe refuge for evacuees. Some of Ripley's unexpected guests, children from a Dr Barnardo's home in London, are seen here listening to a bedtime story read by their 'House Mother' in one of the castle's imposing bedrooms.

Responding to fears that the Germans were planning to use poison gas, the British War Cabinet in 1939 distributed 38 million gas masks. Despite constant exhortations on the BBC to carry these cumbersome devices in their large cardboard boxes at all times, after the initial scare few people could be bothered. In this photograph, Mr W.G. Burton, the headmaster at Topcliffe School near Thirsk, conducts a 'Gas Mask Drill' for his pupils. Children were instructed to spit on the inside of the mica window, to stop it misting up, and then to position the mask over their heads, 'making sure that they insert their chins first'.

At Hedon airfield near Hull RAF crews manhandle torpedoes on to the runway ready for loading.

The Princess Royal, Countess of Harewood (centre), inspects members of the Air Ambulance Corps at Yeadon airfield. The Princess held many public positions and earned great respect for the diligence with which she carried out her duties. Shortly after the war the Princess was given the Freedom of Harrogate and endeared herself even more to the county by declaring, 'If I could live anywhere in the world, it would be here in Yorkshire'.

The long, weary six years of war came to an official end with the proclamation of VJ (Victory over Japan) Day in August 1945. As part of the celebrations at Rotherham rejoicing citizens piled into the coal lighter *Rowland* for a trip along the Don Navigation. In a sense the festivities were premature. Over the next few 'years of austerity' the people of Britain were to experience far more serious shortages of food, fuel and clothing than they had during the war itself.

Rationing of basic commodities continued into the mid-1950s but the Festival of Britain in 1951 and, even more so, the Coronation of Queen Elizabeth II on 2 June 1953 helped raise the spirits of an exhausted nation. At Ripon the children's Coronation float took pride of place in the procession.

At the village of Follifoot, near Harrogate, celebrations took the form of a Coronation tea.

At Kirkbymoorside the townspeople also organized a procession. Marching along with the Rotary Club, the Women's Institute, the Mother's Union and other formal groups was this contingent of gypsies from the encampment at Gillamoor.

The Coronation of Elizabeth II on 2 June 1953 released a tidal wave of optimism. The terrible toll of the Second World War and the grinding austerities of the postwar years were dazzled out of memory by the sumptuous pageantry of that rainy day and by newspaper editorials trumpeting the arrival of a New Elizabethan Age. And Sir Edmund Hillary's conquest of Mount Everest, four days earlier, helped to confirm the feeling that the nation was on the brink of a more confident and prosperous age.

ACKNOWLEDGEMENTS

I am most grateful to the many people across the old Three Ridings who have given me generous assistance in the compilation of this book. I would like to give particular thanks to Mrs J. Pickup who allowed me to plunder her late husband's comprehensive collection of photographs of the former North Riding; to Ken Jackson of 'Memory Lane' in Hull who guided me to some of the most striking images among his hoard of more than 10,000 pictures of the East Riding; and to Mrs Hazel Wheeler in Huddersfield (whose own books on her home town are a delight) for generously loaning me pictures from her personal collection. For assistance in tracking down the stories behind some of the pictures, I am indebted to Anthony Chadwick, Christopher Evans, John Kirkham, G.W. Stevens, George Tattersall-Walker, Dave Walker and to the unfailingly helpful staff at many County Libraries libraries, especially at Bridlington, Ilkley, Northallerton, Pickering and Rotherham. Details are given below of the many sources, private and public, who have contributed to this anthology. My most appreciative thanks to them all.

PICTURE CREDITS

(numbers refer to page numbers)

Author's Collection: 2, 10, 11, 26, 27, 29, 31, 36, 37, 39, 42, 48, 52, 56, 58, 59, 62, 64, 67, 76, 87–9, 91, 98, 99, 104, 109–11, 112–13, 114–16, 117, 120, 123, 126–7, 128–30, 137, 138, 143, 146, 147, 150, 157; Lindsay Balderson, Darlington: 151; Barnardos, Ilford: 45, 56, 57, 66, 153; Beamish Museum: 15, 49, 85, 117, 121, 135, 139, 141; Bridlington Library: 13, 79; Butlin's Holidays Ltd: 105–6; Simon Fitton, Bedale: 148; Harewood House, Leeds: 27, 47, 68, 155; Ken Jackson, 'Memory Lane', Hull: 11, 17, 33, 35, 36, 38, 40–1, 43–4, 62–3, 69, 71, 75, 77, 85, 94, 100, 127, 132–3, 139, 141, 142, 144, 145, 146, 149, 154; Northallerton College: 49–51, 90, 116; Mrs J. Pickup, Pickering: 9, 12, 14, 16, 19, 21–3, 28, 29–30, 31–2, 35, 52, 53, 57, 65, 66, 67, 70, 74, 76, 77, 81, 83, 86, 87, 91, 92, 93, 97, 98, 99, 101–2, 103, 106, 109, 111, 118, 119, 124, 125, 131, 138, 140, 144, 147, 148, 149; Pudsey Civic Society: 14, 74, 102, 118; Harry Ramsden's plc, Guiseley: 78–9; The Right Hon. James Ramsden, Mickley: 117, 134; Rotherham Central Library: 68, 100, 155; John Smiths Brewery, Tadcaster: 81, 82, 92; Ian and Margaret Sumner, Beverley: 13, 21, 37, 73, 97, 119, 124; South Yorkshire County Scout Council, Sheffield: 54–5, 156; The Sutcliffe Gallery, Whitby: 1; Taylors of Harrogate Ltd: 80; Thirsk Museum: 82, 103, 154; Mrs Hazel Wheeler, Huddersfield: 7, 53, 61, 86, 125; Ray Wilkinson, Middleham: 26; Yorkshire Agricultural Society, Harrogate: 24–5, 95; Yorkshire Film Archive, University College of Ripon and York St John: 9, 18, 70, 113, 156.

INDEX